SMART CYCLING

Promoting Safety, Fun, Fitness, and the Environment

League of American Bicyclists

Andy Clarke

Editor

#1 DVD At The Back.

Human Kinetics

Library of Congress Cataloging-in-Publication Data

Smart cycling : promoting safety, fun, fitness, and the environment / League of American Bicyclists, Andy Clarke, editor.
    p. cm.
  Includes bibliographical references and index.
  ISBN-13: 978-0-7360-8717-9 (soft cover)
  ISBN-10: 0-7360-8717-6 (soft cover)
  1. Cycling. 2. Cycling--Equipment and supplies. 3. Cycling--Safety measures. I. Clarke, Andy. II. League of American Bicyclists.
  GV1041.S56 2011
  796.6--dc22

                            2010028587

ISBN-10: 0-7360-8717-6 (print)
ISBN-13: 978-0-7360-8717-9 (print)

Acquisitions Editor: Gayle Kassing, PhD; **Developmental Editor:** Ray Vallese; **Assistant Editor:** Derek Campbell; **Copyeditor:** Mary Rivers; **Indexer:** Bobbi Swanson; **Permission Manager:** Dalene Reeder; **Graphic Designer:** Fred Starbird; **Graphic Artist:** Denise Lowry; **Cover Designer:** Keith Blomberg; **DVD Face Designer:** Susan Rothermel Allen; **Photographer (cover):** Neil Bernstein; **Photographer (interior):** Courtesy of the League of American Bicyclists, unless otherwise noted; **Photo Asset Manager:** Laura Fitch; **Visual Production Assistant:** Joyce Brumfield; **Photo Production Manager:** Jason Allen; **Art Manager:** Kelly Hendren; **Associate Art Manager:** Alan L. Wilborn; **Printer:** Versa Press

The League of American Bicyclists is grateful to Arnie Baker, MD, for the use of the title *Smart Cycling* for this book and for the league's educational curriculum.

Printed in the United States of America   10   9   8   7   6   5   4   3   2   1

The paper in this book is certified under a sustainable forestry program.

Human Kinetics
Web site: www.HumanKinetics.com

United States: Human Kinetics, P.O. Box 5076, Champaign, IL 61825-5076
800-747-4457
e-mail: humank@hkusa.com

Canada: Human Kinetics, 475 Devonshire Road Unit 100, Windsor, ON N8Y 2L5
800-465-7301 (in Canada only)
e-mail: info@hkcanada.com

Europe: Human Kinetics, 107 Bradford Road, Stanningley, Leeds LS28 6AT, United Kingdom
+44 (0) 113 255 5665
e-mail: hk@hkeurope.com

Australia: Human Kinetics, 57A Price Avenue, Lower Mitcham, South Australia 5062
08 8372 0999
e-mail: info@hkaustralia.com

New Zealand: Human Kinetics, P.O. Box 80, Torrens Park, South Australia 5062
0800 222 062
e-mail: info@hknewzealand.com

E4977

CONTENTS

PREFACE

From one of the main modes of transportation in China to a beloved and popular transportation option in the Netherlands, bicycling is a popular and commonplace tradition around the world. In the United States, bicycling had its peaks and valleys throughout the 20th century, and as we end the first decade of the 21st century, its popularity is again soaring. As people seek exercise solutions simpler than joining a gym and look for ways to save money on transportation, bicycling presents an easy option for both. Americans are also coming back to cycling because our country is investing in making it more attractive. Federal transportation funds, as well as state and local investments, are transforming our communities and making it much easier for people who want to ride to do so.

An inspiring example is Portland, Oregon. This city, recognized by the League of American Bicyclists as a platinum-level Bicycle Friendly Community, has spent the past 20 years promoting cycling and investing in infrastructure and education for cyclists. Today, the city's statistics indicate that the number of cyclists in Portland has quadrupled since 1990 while the accident rate has plummeted. (For more information on Portland and the other top 13 U.S. cities for cycling, see appendix B.)

With cities building roads for bicyclists, a bike in almost every garage or shed, and so many good reasons for getting on a bike, the only things missing are the skills and confidence to ride those bikes well with traffic. This book, *Smart Cycling: Promoting Safety, Fun, Fitness, and the Environment,* fills in those missing skills. There have been some exciting changes in cycling in the United States during the past few years. In response to a growing interest in outdoor adventures and increased concern about obesity, bicycling offers a fun and easy way to exercise and explore. This book is a resource for anyone with an interest in bicycling—teachers who want to instruct their students in cycling, recreational center and park employees who want to encourage cycling, and anyone who loves the outdoors. There is also a DVD containing instructional videos on cycling skills and safety for children and adults; for more details, see Using the DVD on page 154.

There is a good deal of instruction in this book, from how to signal correctly to emergency maneuvers you may need to know in a tricky situation. Bicycles are considered vehicles in all 50 states, and their riders must observe the same rules of the road as do the drivers of any other vehicle. Because cyclists' size and speed relative to cars and trucks have the potential for dangerous crashes, this book offers tips and techniques on safely and correctly riding with traffic.

The most important message in *Smart Cycling,* though, is this: Cycling is open to everyone, is a great way to get around, and is a lot of fun. If you want to invest thousands of dollars in a bike and get outfitted in the latest spandex gear, that's fine. If you want to resurrect the abandoned bike in your garage, take it to a bike shop to get it up to speed, and then ride it around town in shorts and a T-shirt, that's fine too. Cycling is an equal-opportunity adventure, open to anyone willing to pedal uphill, coast downhill, and enjoy all the moments in between.

The book is especially aimed at educators and others who teach children. A 2010 study by the Kaiser Family Foundation found that 8- to 18-year-olds spend an average of 7 hours and 38 minutes using entertainment media (cell phones, television, video games) in a typical day. Rather than stay indoors connected to electronics, children need to be outdoors, able to explore and learn independence. A bicycle can be the vehicle that opens an entire new world to them. Reversing the downward trend of children who bicycle to school is an important part of the mission of this book, but children must be ready to ride on the road. The techniques in this book are specifically designed to help children and adults use bicycles safely as transportation.

Protecting the environment is also on everyone's mind: encouraging people to reuse bags at the supermarket, to compost, to drive fewer miles, and so on. Bicycling is an easy way to sharply lower carbon emissions while sharply increasing fun. Going green can feel a bit overwhelming—remembering to take those bags back to the market is a heroic effort in and of itself!—but bicycling is an easy and fun way to reduce the environmental footprint. Saving money on fuel and other vehicle-related expenses is another benefit.

This book was written in cooperation with the League of American Bicyclists (hereafter referred to as the league). The league was founded as the League of American Wheelmen in 1880. Bicyclists, known then as "wheelmen," were challenged by rutted roads of gravel and dirt and faced antagonism from horsemen, wagon drivers, and pedestrians. In an effort to improve riding conditions so they might better enjoy their newly discovered sport, more than 100,000 cyclists from across the United States joined the league to advocate for paved roads. The success of the league in its first advocacy efforts played a role in the national highway system.

Today, the league still advocates for cyclists in the nation's capital and across the country. In addition to advocacy work, the league promotes cycling, educates cyclists and motorists on sharing the road, and works to build a bicycle-friendly America. At www.bikeleague.org, you can find information on our education programs (such as this book); our recognition program through which businesses, communities, and states earn the Bicycle Friendly designation; and our national advocacy work in Washington, DC.

This guide will allow you to master the art of cycling as well as teach it to others. The information in this book has been tested on the road by hundreds of thousands of cyclists. Enjoy the ride!

ACKNOWLEDGMENTS

In 2004, the League of American Bicyclists self-published *A Guide to Safe and Enjoyable Cycling*. The book was our first real attempt to popularize the content of the league's education program, then called simply BikeEd, and share with a wider audience the helpful, practical, and potentially life-saving tips and techniques for riding a bike safely in traffic. The book was written by staff and volunteers over several years and was an important step forward for the organization and the subject matter.

The book has served us well—but the opportunity to update the material, include a particular focus on children, and publish the book with Human Kinetics was timely and most welcome. The additional rigor with which the material has been checked and double-checked by Gayle, Ray, Derek, and the team at Human Kinetics has been both essential and illuminating. The league's education director, Preston Tyree, has ensured we stick close to the core principles of our education program—now called Smart Cycling—which is taught by thousands of league-certified instructors across the country; and colleagues Anna Kelso and David Herlihy graciously contributed "Cycling for the Fun of It" and the history section of "History and Benefits of Bicycling," respectively.

Smart Cycling would not have happened without the leadership and commitment of Elizabeth Kiker on the league's staff. She has tirelessly shepherded the book through stages of publication some of us didn't realize even existed and has painstakingly pulled together the pictures, graphs, and references so that we all end up looking good.

Finally, the inspiration for a book like this has to be the next generation of riders. My own children, Jacqueline and Ashton, are already avid riders to and from school and around the neighborhood—and I hope this book will encourage them to reach even further afield a-wheel. Elizabeth's kids, Oliver and Allyson, are a little younger and have a year or two more of being carried around by Mom, but their time will soon come when they too can learn the simple pleasure of a bike ride and enjoy it more safely.

HISTORY AND BENEFITS OF BICYCLING

When I see an adult on a bicycle,
I do not despair for the future of the human race.

—H.G. Wells

It took hundreds of years for bicycles to develop from the idea of human-powered transit to the fun, easy vehicles seen everywhere today. Inventors, passionate cyclists, and creative thinkers all played a part in the development of the bicycle. Today's bicycles, the result of all this hard work, provide cyclists with a great way to lose weight, improve their mental health, and help the environment.

HISTORY OF BICYCLING

"History of Bicycling" contributed by David Herlihy

More than three centuries ago, the distinguished French mathematician Jacques Ozanam recognized the compelling theoretical advantages of a human-powered carriage "in which one can drive oneself wherever one pleases, without horses." The modern bicycle, a remarkably efficient and economical machine, is in effect the culmination of an ancient quest to design and build a practical vehicle propelled by that abundant resource known as willpower.

By the early 19th century, the Industrial Revolution was picking up steam, energizing inventors of all stripes. In 1813, Karl von Drais, an eccentric German baron from a distinguished family in Karlsruhe, built a four-wheeled vehicle seating up to four passengers. Several passengers supplied the power by working a cranked axle with their legs, while another steered by means of a tiller. Convinced that he had finally achieved a practical horseless carriage, Drais courted the public's approval. Several journals published descriptions, and a few luminaries offered accolades, notably the Russian tsar, Alexander I. Still, the patent offices of both Austria and his native Baden rejected his pleas for protection. One examiner even issued a harsh rebuke, insisting that no man-made device could ever improve on the God-given means of walking.

A few years later, in 1817, Drais proposed a radically different solution: the laufmaschine (running machine), a personalized vehicle soon to be known as a draisine or velocipede (from the Latin words meaning fast foot) (figure 1.1). It represented the first significant step toward the basic bicycle, a compact, pedal-powered vehicle.

Except for its iron tires, the machine was made almost entirely of wood and had but two miniature carriage wheels in a line, connected by a perch that supported a single cushioned seat. The rider sat nearly erect and propelled the machine by pushing off the ground with one foot, then the other, as if walking or running. A long pole pivoted at the foremost end of the frame, allowing the rider to turn the front wheel in the desired direction of travel. A small padded board was affixed waist high in front of the seat, on which the rider could rest the elbows or forearms, shifting pressure as needed to keep the vehicle from tipping to one side or the other.

Emergence of the Basic Bicycle

For the next few decades, inventors continued to toy with velocipedes, generally reverting to four-wheeled platforms while proposing all sorts of propulsion schemes that employed either the legs or arms, or both (figure 1.2). Some, like Willard Sawyer of Dover, England, even enjoyed modest commercial success. Still, the

Figure 1.1   The 1818 British patent of Denis Johnson, a coach builder in London, describes an improved kick-propelled two-wheeled velocipede.

Courtesy of the National Archives (Northeast Branch, New York)

public continued to regard the velocipede as a failure with, at best, dim prospects for improvement.

Finally, in the mid-1860s, the basic bicycle emerged in Paris. The brainchild of Pierre Lallement, a mechanic who specialized in baby carriages, it strongly resembled the hobby horse except for the pedals protruding from the front hub. The slender vehicle reprised Drais' delightfully compact profile. At the same time, it demonstrated the surprising principle that a vehicle with but two wheels in a line could be indefinitely balanced and propelled by means of a mechanical drive—rather than by human propulsion alone. This removed the principal objection to the draisine and opened a promising path for development.

Lallement himself, meanwhile, had emigrated to Connecticut with the makings of an improved bicycle in tow (figure 1.3). In the spring of 1866, he tooled around New

Figure 1.2 One of the many unsuccessful attempts to build a practical human-powered vehicle after the demise of the draisine and before the introduction of the basic bicycle.

Courtesy of the Boston Public Library

Haven, to the amazement of a journalist who reported the next day: "An enterprising individual propelled himself about the Green last evening on a curious frame sustained by two wheels, one before the other, and driven by foot cranks" (as recounted in "Pierre Lallement and His Bicycle," *Wheelmen Illustrated,* Oct. 1883). Lallement's antics attracted an investor, James Carroll, and the two were soon awarded an American patent, the world's first published document describing the basic bicycle.

They failed, nevertheless, to enlist a manufacturer and a dejected Lallement returned to Paris. To his great surprise, however, he found that the Michaux bicycle had become a great hit there in his absence. The novelty also caught the attention of foreign visitors, including Americans who began to take an interest in the machine.

Bicycles in America

The "boneshaker" (so nicknamed because the wooden wheels were very tough on riders) unleashed a frenzy of experimentation and fired the public's imagination. "Never before in the history of manufacturers in this country," marveled the *New York Times* in early 1869, "has there arisen such a demand for an article."

In the interim, however, the crude bicycle spawned the majestic high-wheeler. Developed primarily in France and England, the new design retained the boneshaker's simple but effective direct drive. Its enlarged front wheel, meanwhile, gave a better gear. Its vastly improved construction, employing wire wheels, ball bearings, and tubular frames, halved the weight of the typical bicycle and gave a much better ride. The new vehicle could now travel a hundred miles in a single day, even over poor dirt roads.

By the mid-1870s, the new style of bicycle had gained a significant following among prosperous young Englishmen who relished camaraderie and adventure on the open road. By the end of that decade, exploiting the Lallement patent, the

Figure 1.3   Pierre Lallement poses on a velocipede in Paris in 1869 or 1870. After returning to France he sold his patent and used the funds to start a short-lived bicycle business.
Courtesy of the Library of Congress

Boston businessman Albert A. Pope reigned over a robust American cycle industry. For all its appeal, however, the high bicycle was intimidating to untold numbers of would-be cyclists. It often catapulted the rider over the handlebars, at times causing serious injury and even death. The industry came under increased pressure to offer safer alternatives (figure 1.4).

Although several other designs, including tricycles, gained a small following in the 1880s, it was the Rover that would set the fashion for the world by the end of that decade. Developed by J.K. Starley of Coventry, England, the so-called safety bicycle featured wheels of equal size, the rear one powered by a chain and sprocket. By the early 1890s, with the introduction of inflatable tires, the upstart bicycle, eerily reminiscent of the old boneshaker, had driven the high-wheelers off the road while attracting legions of new riders, including women.

A great boom exploded as millions the world over took to the feather-light wheel, weighing a scant 25 pounds. Gushed one American in the August 1895 issue of *The Cosmopolitan,* "It is well nigh impossible to calculate the far-reaching effects of [the bicycle's] influence." For starters, the low-mount safety bicycle encouraged an increasingly sedentary population to exercise outdoors. The bicycle also had an enormous impact on women and the rigid Victorian dress code. "Since women have taken up the bicycle," noted one feminist, "it has become more and more apparent that its use demands a radical change in costume" (*The Cosmopolitan,* August 1895). Some even began to use the bicycle for everyday transportation.

Figure 1.4 An American Star being driven down the Capitol steps in the late 1880s to show its superior stability relative to the high-wheeler. For a brief time, Star became a favorite among American cycle tourists and racers.
Courtesy of the Library of Congress

Still, the bicycle did not truly complete its transition from a rich man's toy to a poor man's carriage until the early part of the 20th century. Before the boom, the first safety bicycles had cost about $150—at a time when the average worker made only about $12 a week. And despite its popularity, it remained a costly investment throughout the boom. But shortly thereafter, reliable bicycles were selling for only around $25, primarily through department stores and mail-order houses.

Bicycling Around the World

Throughout the 1920s and 1930s, utilitarian and recreational cycling thrived in Europe. The touring bicycle, developed primarily in France and England, used light-weight frames, aluminum alloy parts, and hub or derailleur gears. Cycle camping became popular among the middle class, while a growing network of youth hostels, born in Germany, offered cycle tourists cheap accommodations.

In developing countries like India and China, demand for utilitarian bicycles soared. In the car-crazy United States, meanwhile, the bicycle had become primarily a child's vehicle, laden with automotive-style gadgets. However, in the midst of the Great Depression, the country suddenly experienced a brisk recreational revival, taking a cue from Hollywood actors like Joan Crawford who had discovered the joys of cycling. The bicycles, patterned after children's models, were nonetheless heavy, weighing a good 50 pounds or more.

During World War II, the bicycle played an even larger role in everyday life in Europe. Even fuel-pinched Americans turned to the two-wheeler for basic transportation. Although reliance on the bicycle would wane at the conclusion of the conflict, recreational interest enjoyed another revival, thanks in large part to the flood of GIs who returned from Europe with a greater appreciation for lightweight bicycles with three-speed hub gears.

In the late 1960s, following a juvenile fad for the low-riding, fast-moving Schwinn Sting-Ray, American adults began to acquire a taste for even lighter and more versatile bicycles with derailleurs, known as 10-speeds. A second boom occurred. Suppliers in Europe, Asia, and America worked frantically to meet the overwhelming demand, selling some 40 million bicycles between 1972 and 1974. Although sales eventually tapered off, cycling had reestablished itself on both sides of the Atlantic as a popular adult pastime.

Since then, the versatile mountain bike, with fat tires and multiple gears, has given cycling a wonderful boost. In the late 1970s, a group of young men and women based in Marin County, California, began to modify old bicycles for off-road use. By the 1980s, manufacturers had recognized a market for rugged yet comfortable bicycles that could go just about anywhere. The robust design of the mountain bike, conducive to city riding, has also been a boon to utilitarian cyclists, spawning the wildly popular hybrid bicycle. Hybrids have wider tires and an upright position, like mountain bikes, and include the larger wheel size of road bikes. Their versatility allows riders to use them on road, trails, and some off-road situations.

Bicycling Today

Today, the bicycle continues to provide cheap and clean transportation. Of course, it is still widely used throughout the developing world, even as many countries strive to increase domestic automobile production and sales. In developed countries, the bicycle is increasingly favored as a "green" machine that can help reduce obesity and traffic congestion. Many cities now offer extensive bicycle lanes and even sophisticated rental networks. Many firms encourage bicycle commuting to improve the health of their employees.

Recreational cycling is also on the rise: Consumers enjoy a greater variety of cycles than ever before at all price points. Many consider RAGBRAI (which stands for Register's Annual Great Bicycle Ride Across Iowa) the start of cross-state tours. From its inception in 1973, there are now more than 20,000 participants in the week-long ride, each of whom pay only $140. On the other end of the spectrum, Cycle Oregon is a plush, tightly organized ride that limits itself to 2,000 riders. This allows them to treat each rider like royalty, serving excellent food, microbrews, and much more. The joy of Cycle Oregon will set you back $850, and it sells out within a week of the

BICYCLE FRIENDLY AMERICA

The League of American Bicyclists' Bicycle Friendly America program teaches, rewards, and encourages bicycling in America. The program recognizes businesses, communities, and states for promoting and supporting cycling. Awards given are bronze, silver, gold, and platinum—all are coveted designations. Visit www.bikeleague.org to find out more.

Bicycle Friendly Businesses

The Bicycle Friendly Business (BFB) program recognizes employers' efforts to encourage a more bicycle-friendly atmosphere for employees and customers. The program honors innovative bike-friendly efforts and provides technical assistance and information to help companies and organizations become even better for bicyclists.

Bicycle Friendly Communities

The **Bicycle Friendly Community** (BFC) application is an in-depth audit of the engineering, education, encouragement, enforcement, and evaluation efforts in a municipality. This comprehensive inquiry is designed to yield a holistic picture of a community's work to promote bicycling. The application is free, and assistance is available from league staff members.

Bicycle Friendly States

The Bicycle Friendly State program is a two-part recognition program that ranks and recognizes states that actively support bicycling. First, states are ranked annually based on their level of bike-friendliness. Secondly, states that wish to apply for a Bicycle Friendly State award designation can receive further recognition and promotion of their efforts as well as feedback, technical assistance, training, and further encouragement to improve their bicycling legislation, projects, and programs.

opening. Scores of organizations host annual rides to raise money for charities and cycling clubs abound. The Multiple Sclerosis Society hosts rides across the United States that raise millions of dollars, as do the American Diabetes Association, Bike and Build, the Lance Armstrong Foundation, and many more. These rides are fun and raise hundreds of millions of dollars for charity.

Since bicycling was first included in the U.S. transportation bill in 1991, federal, state, and local funding for bicycling has blossomed. In the decades since, communities have paved old railroad lines to become trails, added bike lanes to miles of streets, and developed single-track trails for mountain bicyclists.

Where will the bicycle go from here? Some believe it is due for a major overhaul, given the superior speed of low-slung aerodynamic models known as recumbents, where riders are seated and their legs are straight out in front of them. Others predict the most popular bicycle of the future will have an electric motor, ready to kick in whenever the riders' will to pedal wanes. A 2010 article in the *New York Times* notes that there are currently an estimated 120 million electric bicycles on the streets of China, up from a few thousand in the 1990s (Goodman 2010). Regardless of what lies ahead, the bicycle's rich and colorful history projects a future as bright and energetic as its past.

BENEFITS OF BICYCLING

The bicycle is a simple two-wheeled machine that uses human power for propulsion. But riding this machine is one of the great and simple joys of life. It grants a sense of delight and accomplishment no matter your age or ability—from a 3-year-old on training wheels to an 85-year-old riding 50 miles in a day. The wind in your face and the freedom with which you flow over the earth can refresh the soul. Your heart pounds, and your muscles push you faster and faster up a hill. Then, as you stop pedaling and coast down the other side, a grin magically spreads across your face.

Of course, the benefits of bicycling include more than freedom and independence. Cycling helps you save money on fuel, get into better shape, and remain healthier longer. Bicycling is a fitness activity that the entire family can enjoy together. Bicycles are used for recreation, transportation, sport, and work. In fact, more people around the world use the bicycle as a means of transportation than any other vehicle (Did You Know? n.d.). Starting at below $100, the bicycle is a form of transportation virtually everyone can afford and a way of life that no one should pass up.

Lose Weight, Gain Fitness

The bicycle offers an enormous range of practical benefits for individuals, families, and society as a whole. Bicycling is one of the best activities for the cardiovascular system, and cycling is very effective for reducing weight and keeping it off. A 150-pound cyclist burns 410 calories in 1 hour while pedaling at a moderate pace of 12 miles per hour—burning the number of calories nearly equivalent to a plate of pasta with Alfredo sauce. A 200-pound cyclist burns 708 calories in 1 hour while pedaling at 12 miles an hour—burning calories equivalent to that of a lean steak with a baked potato and serving of broccoli (NutriStrategy 2005).

Get Mentally Healthy

Bicycling is good not only for the body but also for the mind. In addition to breathing fresh air and exercising, the cyclist is his own vehicle, using self-power instead of machine power to get from point A to point B. This is a remarkably good feeling—to ride by the bus parked in traffic, glide past the cars stopped on the road as you coast by on a trail, or arrive at work powered by nothing but your own legs. These achievements help frame each day as successful from the beginning. Bicycling also relaxes you, giving you time to think as you ride, reducing your stress levels, and increasing your self-esteem and self-confidence as you improve.

Bike to School

Bicycling remains a popular activity among children and a way to stay active and healthy for all ages, but it has declined as a functional mode of transport. According

Kid's-Eye View

The Benefits of Bicycling

Kids are battling obesity at even higher rates than adults in the United States; daily activity is an important prescription to change this. How do you know if your child is ready to ride a bicycle? Here are some tips:

- Once a child can hold up his head and wear a helmet, he can be a passenger on a bike.
- Until about age five, kids should ride in a child seat, or better yet, a trailer.
- Kids need basic motor skills to operate a bike.

If kids are ready, be sure to teach them about riding safely:

- Explain to kids how traffic works; they have only been passengers.
- Teach them about yielding, passing, predicting, and obeying traffic laws.
- Bicycle riders have to obey the same rules as cars and buses.

to the National Household Travel Survey, funded by the Federal Highway Administration, in the 1960s more than 40 percent of children bicycled and walked to school (sometimes "uphill both ways in the snow"!). Today, only 12 percent of children bike or walk to school. At the same time, a survey done by the Centers for Disease Control and Prevention (n.d.) shows children are fighting obesity and diseases at unprecedented rates. About 32 percent of American children and adolescents today—25 million kids—are obese or overweight, according to the survey, and diseases such as type 2 diabetes (known previously as adult-onset diabetes) and asthma are becoming more common. A return to biking to school could help combat some of these serious conditions and diseases. The national legislation creating the Safe Routes to School was passed in 2005 and allocated $612 million to programs that encourage children to walk and bike to school.

Start Your Day Right by Commuting

According to the 2009 Nationwide Personal Transportation Survey, 28 percent of all trips in the United States are a mile or less, and 40 percent of all trips are two miles or less. Though these distances can easily be traveled by bike, more than 72 percent of trips within three miles of home are made by personal motor vehicle. These statistics could radically change if more people chose to bicycle to work (figure 1.5).

People who commute to work by bike, rather than car, avoid stress-inducing traffic jams, tollbooth lines, and battles for parking spots. They arrive at work feeling energized instead of enervated. They are ready to work, not frustrated

Figure 1.5 Commuting to work, and enjoying fresh air and companionship, is a great way to start and end your day.

and in need of a break. Bicycle commuters often find they save time because they can breeze past traffic and do not need to hunt for a parking space for a vehicle. Generally, a bicycle commuter can easily find parking space for his bike. Bike commuters also get great exercise while cycling to work, saving the time and expense of health club workouts. In addition, bicycle commuters also save a small fortune in gasoline and automobile maintenance and repairs. In fact, many people who regularly commute by bicycle have found that their family can go from two cars to one, saving hundreds of dollars per month in auto and insurance payments. Some northern cities, including Minneapolis, Minnesota, and Madison, Wisconsin, are so good about plowing and keeping the trails and roads safe for cyclists that people ride year-round. That kind of dedication isn't necessary for everyone, though, and actually many cyclists don't have the equipment necessary to ride in a downpour or snow. However, it isn't necessary to bike in bad weather to enjoy the many benefits of commuting by bike.

Help the Environment

Bicycling gets you where you need to go without burning fossil fuels, emitting pollutants, or increasing traffic congestion. According to Sorenson and the Sightline Institute (2008), "The bicycle—the most energy-efficient form of travel ever devised—deserves better. Pound for pound, a person on a bicycle expends less energy than any creature or machine covering the same distance. (A human walking spends about three times as much energy per pound; even a salmon swimming spends about twice as much.)" Cycling is a means for an excellent aerobic workout while traveling, as long as you are pedaling hard enough to get your heart rate up. After walking, bicycling is the most widely used form of transportation in the world.

MORE PEOPLE ARE RIDING

More and more people are realizing—and experiencing—the many benefits of cycling. A 2002 survey titled National Survey of Pedestrian and Bicyclist Attitudes and Behaviors from the National Bureau of Statistics found that 28 percent of adults, 57 million people, rode a bicycle during the previous summer. Of the 72 percent who did not ride, only 6.5 percent stated that they did not like to ride. The two most popular reasons cited for not riding were lack of time and the lack of access to a bike. This suggests that with some inducement (in the form of community programming and outreach) and more promotion of bicycling to work, those numbers could increase dramatically. Since that time, cycling levels in cities across the country have increased by 48 percent (U.S. Census Bureau 2008) and even more in cities such as New York, Chicago, Seattle, and Washington, DC that have actively promoted bicycling.

FIVE STEPS TO RIDING BETTER

1. Follow the rules of the road.
2. Be visible.
3. Be predictable.
4. Anticipate conflicts.
5. Wear a helmet.

League of American Bicyclists, n.d.

CONCLUSION

From the push-yourself-along draisine to the high-wheeler of yesterday, it took more than a century to create a modern safety bicycle. Today's bicycle is an engineering marvel, honed over the past century to be a light, easy, and fast way to get around. The benefits of cycling are enormous, from improved health to leaving a smaller environmental footprint. Riding a bicycle burns calories, saves money, conserves energy, and (the best reason of all) is a lot of fun.

CHAPTER 2

CHOOSING A BICYCLE

T here are two elements for bicycle riding: a bicycle and you. People use their bikes for many different activities. They may ride around the neighborhood or on paved trails, commute to and from work, and run errands. People use bikes for sport, including road and trail riding; others load up their bikes and tour the country on two wheels. Identifying how you will use your bike will help you immensely when considering what type to buy. Your budget will probably play a primary factor in your bike selection; other factors include style, construction quality, and the feel of the ride. This chapter discusses the kinds of bikes available and the types of riding people generally do, and then it offers pointers on choosing a bike.

CONNECTING RIDING STYLES TO BIKES

While all bikes are generally the same, with a seat (saddle), two wheels, and a frame, there are many variables that affect the type of bicycle appropriate for you. From upright bikes with internal gears designed for city riding to single-speed racing bikes, there is a wide variety of bikes currently on the market. The following section is an introduction to the most common bikes and the differences between them.

Mountain Bikes

With fat, low-pressure tires and durable frames, mountain bikes are designed for off-road riding, through gravel and dirt, and over rocks and roots (figure 2.1). Because the tires on mountain bikes use less pressure than road bike tires, they offer the rider a little bit of shock absorption and greater traction. A wide gear range enables you to climb steep grades. Powerful brakes, shifters at your fingertips, and upright or flat handlebars provide control and stability. Front and rear suspension can smooth out the bumps in the trail.

Figure 2.1 Mountain bike, designed for off-road riding.

Multipurpose mountain bikes are popular and offer off-road versatility, but they have less city-riding functionality. Knobby tires give more rolling resistance, which makes them harder to ride on the road. They are designed for use off road. Mountain bikes have smaller frame dimensions and are easier and more stable to corner and maneuver over curbs and rocks. They generally feature 26-inch wheels and wide (1- to 2.5-inch) tires. Because the frame geometry is frequently more compact, with sloping top tubes and short wheelbases, attaching commuting gear to a mountain bike may be more difficult. In addition, the rider's position leans forward more aggressively. This may put the rider in a less upright position than that of a comfort bike. These bikes are often the perfect selection for children and younger adults because they are fun, versatile, and usually the least expensive bikes in a shop.

Like any bike, mountain bikes can be used for town riding or commuting, but not all the special features found on a nice mountain bike enhance a city ride. Many competitive mountain bike frames are small, designed for ease in maneuverability, not comfort, and the shocks can slow a bike down and add unnecessary weight.

Road (Racing) Bikes

Road bikes are designed to be ridden on smooth surfaces (figure 2.2). Built for speed, with narrow, smooth high-pressure tires, the road bike is a highly efficient ride. The drop handlebars (or **drop bars**, curved in the shape of a ram's horn) let you adjust your position to achieve maximum efficiency while climbing, descending, or relaxing. Wheel rims tend to be made of lightweight material—strong, but not ideal for carrying large loads or riding rough terrain. The wheels on a road bike are generally called 700c, which is an old French measurement that means they are a little smaller than 27 inches in diameter. This is a typical wheel size for working-

Figure 2.2 Road (racing) bike, designed for speed and agility on the road. This road bike is outfitted with aero bars.

class bikes around the world, although some road bikes come with 650c wheels. Road bikes adapted for triathlons (competitions involving three races: swimming, biking, and running) are designed with steeper seat tube angles to bring the rider into an even more aggressive and powerful position and are often outfitted with accessories such as aero bars (handlebars or handlebar attachments that allow the rider to assume a lower, more aerodynamic upper-body position; see figure 2.2) and bladed spokes (spokes that have been flattened for increased aerodynamics) that decrease wind resistance.

Racing bikes are designed for speed and position a cyclist in a competitive, compact position. High-end racing bikes are intended to be very light, wind resistant, responsive to each pedal stroke, and easy for skilled riders to turn and corner quickly. Racing bike wheels can be very stiff and somewhat fragile, with extremely skinny, high-pressure tires to reduce rolling resistance, sometimes even at the expense of overall handling quality.

Racing bikes are fun and fast, but they often lack the ability to be used as a practical city bike because they won't accept fenders or racks that hold bags. Their compact design makes the road bike less comfortable than most bikes on short rides; often the high-pressure tires are also less forgiving on urban pavement. In addition, while the quality of racing bikes varies greatly, these bikes are among the most expensive bikes and thus a target of bike thieves. Some people just don't want to put wear and tear on their expensive weekend bike by riding around town, in bad weather, or on rough roads with pot holes. However, for people who like road bikes, one commuter solution is to buy an older road bike for city riding. Used bikes can sometimes be found at excellent prices.

Comfort (Hybrid) Bikes

These all-purpose bikes borrow features from both mountain and road bikes (figure 2.3). From the mountain bike, the comfort bike takes the wide gear range, upright riding position, and powerful brakes. Like a road bike, comfort bikes feature higher-pressure, medium-width tires that make for an efficient and comfortable ride.

Comfort-style bikes, or hybrids, have become popular in the United States. Comfort bikes are easy to mount and dismount; have an upright, comfortable position; and can accommodate baskets, bags, and commuting gear. Comfort bikes are not high-performance bikes; they are often heavier and less agile, but they can still handle high speeds and packed dirt paths. Because of increased popularity, there is a wide variety of styles and prices. Even expert bikers and racers can be found on cool comfort bikes for commuting and weekend jaunts. They generally have 700c wheels and flat handlebars as opposed to drop bars. They often have a wide range of gears for a variety of terrain.

Touring Bikes

Touring bikes are road bikes that have special features for long-distance or overnight travel (figure 2.4). These include racks for carrying heavy gear, a longer wheelbase for a more stable ride, lower gearing to make climbing easier, and often fenders. Touring bikes are designed to provide a more relaxed position for the rider for long days in the saddle.

A touring bike can be a perfect commuting bike because of its ability to hold gear and its durability and stability. Touring bikes are often made of vibration-damping

Figure 2.3 Comfort (hybrid) bike, designed for an easy, relaxed style of riding, usually around town.

Figure 2.4 Touring bike, designed for long rides and great comfort.

steel, which is very sturdy and able to handle bumps and even endure falls. Touring bikes can generally take fatter tires that provide good traction on wet and slick pavement, have strong and sturdy brakes, and have forks wide enough to accommodate fenders. These bikes are still responsive and can meet the need for performance.

Because touring bikes are a combination of road bike and hybrid, and because they tend to be more expensive than other types of bikes, they are purchased less frequently. Therefore, there are fewer choices in a new touring bike. In fact, a new touring bike can be priced higher than most other bikes due to supply and demand. But generally, touring bikes have quality components and are well crafted. As with racing bikes, finding a nice, used touring bike can be a perfect commuting bike alternative, although it can be more difficult to find a used touring bike than a used racing bike.

Recumbent Bikes

On a **recumbent bike**, riders sit in a reclined, or recumbent, position and pedal with their legs in front of their body (figure 2.5). Recumbents are available in a variety of shapes and sizes, with two to four wheels, and under- or overseat steering. Many recumbent riders tout the comfort of the seated position while others enjoy the wind-cheating abilities of these bikes. The seating position on these bikes is part of what many consider their best and worst qualities. Because recumbent riders are seated low and in a more aerodynamic position than other bikes, they are able to gain great speeds on downhills, work harder on uphills, and generally fly on flat roads. This position also makes them harder to spot on the road, which is why many recumbents have flags, banners, and brightly colored decorations on them. The recumbent's wide frame can be an issue when riding on trails.

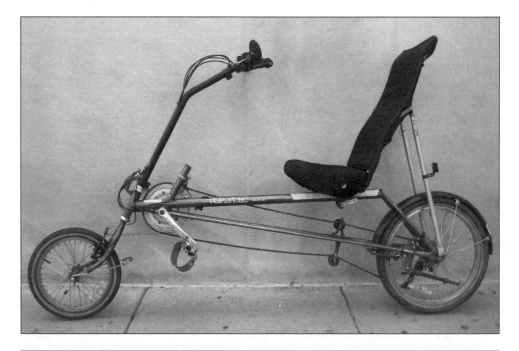

Figure 2.5 Recumbent bikes, which come in a variety of shapes and sizes, can be very comfortable to ride.

Similar to touring bikes, recumbent bikes tend to be purchased by experienced cyclists who know what they want. There is a lot of variety within them, including some tricycle versions, but they all start at a higher price point than mountain or hybrid bikes.

Commuter Bikes

Many people who bicycle to work or school adapt one of the above styles of bikes to their needs, but the true commuter or city bike should have a bell or horn, fenders, durable wheels and tires, a front white light and a rear red light, a cargo rack, panniers, and powerful brakes (figure 2.6). While any bicycle can be turned into a commuter bike by adding these features, in the past 10 years, companies like Breezer and Trek have started selling bikes designed specifically for commuting. These bikes already have lights (usually powered by a generator), racks, and fenders.

If commuting is the main purpose of a bike, buying one already outfitted with these features saves time and money. Alternatively, the great thing about commuting by bicycle is that any style of bike can quickly and easily become a commuter bike.

Figure 2.6 Commuter bikes, including lights, fenders, and a rack, are designed for getting to work easily and quickly.

Other Types of Bikes

There is a wide range of other types of bicycles available. For example, tandem bikes are designed so that two people, in close cooperation, can ride together. Different tandems are designed for riding on- or off-road, as well as for recumbent cycling. In addition, other types of bikes include **BMX** (bicycle motocross) and trial bikes for jumps and other stunts, cyclocross bikes with knobby road-sized tires, track bikes with single fixed gears, tricycles for adults who can't use standard bicycles, beach cruisers, trailer bikes for children, and more. A number of bicycle manufacturers have also introduced bikes in a variety of styles that are specifically designed to fit a woman's body, with shorter top tube lengths and a variety of components specifically made for women.

TUNING UP YOUR OLD BIKE

You may decide to rescue a bike from the deepest recesses of your garage. Possibly an old bike meets your riding needs and only needs to be tuned up. If that is the case, make sure the bike fits you properly (see the section on bicycle fit, p. 28). Then visit the bike shop for a safety inspection or, more likely, a tune-up, to help avoid potentially dangerous malfunctions and make sure your ride is as enjoyable as possible.

If your garage bike needs serious work to make it road worthy and safe, compare the price of a full tune-up with a new bike. After new tires, new chain, a full tune-up, and the possible replacement of other defunct parts, you may find that a new bike that totally suits your needs is comparable in price and perhaps the better choice.

RIDING STYLES

People of all ages use bicycles for many reasons. Young children often use the bike to ride around the block. As they get older and their skills develop, they may start riding to school, local parks, the library, or ball games. College students often use bikes, since college campuses have limited parking, and students may be on a shoestring budget. As we get older, our bike use may change to include commuting to work and taking the family on a Sunday ride. Many adults use bikes for serious recreation, competition, touring, or work.

What type of riding do you do or would you like to do? If you have a clear answer to this question, you may already have a bike of some sort. If so, do you enjoy riding your current bike? Does it meet your needs? If, however, you are just beginning to ride or just exploring your options, selecting your first bike might be a little more difficult, necessitating trade-offs between comfort, durability, versatility, and speed.

Types of Cyclists

For those of you who are getting back into cycling, the best thing you can do is simply get back on a bike. If you have friends who ride, you might initially try to borrow a bike and ride with them to benefit from their encouragement and support. Many people who haven't ridden a bike in a long time are concerned about the dangers of riding in traffic, so start by exploring low-traffic neighborhoods or riding in a park closed to motor vehicles or on a multiuse trail.

You may also have preconceived notions about what you will use a bike for, such as bike commuting, recreational riding, or running errands. These ideas will help you identify your needs so that when you go into a bike shop, you can test ride the appropriate bike type. If you don't have a bike to try out and are unsure what type of riding you want to do, it might be difficult to find the right bike your first time.

Many adults who are getting back into riding ask for a bike that will handle many situations but will be used mostly for casual recreation and slow city riding. According to the National Bicycle Dealers Association (2009), bike shops have seen tremendous growth in sales of comfort and hybrid bikes. Entry-level mountain bikes and, most notably, comfort bikes can meet most requests for diversity, style, and comfort at a reasonable cost.

As you start to cycle more frequently, you can home in on your likely needs. Many people start commuting and using a bike for errands. Often you can make simple adjustments to your bike, such as adding a rack, bike bags, a basket, fenders, and lights to make it a utility bike. Others have the need for speed or want to play on single-track trails, and their entry-level bike might not be best suited for them.

If you are an intermediate cyclist, you can more easily assess what type of riding you do, determine whether your bike meets your needs, and decide if you desire more equipment and gear to meet an expanded range of needs. There is nothing wrong with gear, but being thoughtful about your first bike purchase can help you avoid spending extra money.

Once you fall in love with cycling, you will probably start using your bicycle for a great many other uses. You may go on longer day rides, perhaps 20 to 100 miles. You may also enjoy riding off-road on rocks and roots, and you may bike to work every week. Again, while there are bikes that can handle all of these activities, the desirability and practicality of having two or more bikes will grow.

Multipurpose Riding

Multipurpose bicycling is common among many bicyclists, from beginners to pros. People start riding around the neighborhood, take a bike to a paved bike trail, take a bike with them to ride while on vacation at the beach, ride their bike to work, and bike to the shops on Sunday. Multipurpose bicyclists should strongly consider a practical, comfortable bike. Road bikes, touring bikes, hybrids, or mountain bikes can all be put to multiple uses. Personal preference, budget, and riding style will determine which bike you choose. Your main bike should meet 70 percent of your needs, and then you can decide if you want to add bikes for special uses.

Commuting and Transportation

Commuting is one specific use that the multipurpose bikers may find themselves engaging in frequently. Many people who use a bike for urban transportation and making trips want a higher-performance ride, mainly a bike with a road frame. A touring bike is a common road bike for commuters.

Commuters may use an older, slightly dinged-up bike to deter theft and reduce stress over inevitable scratches. Errand bikes in Europe and Asia are usually of this type, traditionally looking more like comfort bikes with heavy-duty frames, racks, baskets, and fenders. Such commuter bikes usually only have one or two gears. These and other single-speed "cruiser" models are becoming more popular in the United States as well.

Longer Rides

Once you start to ride farther and more frequently, perhaps going on a group bike ride, tour, or a fully supported adventure ride, you will begin to realize that your comfort bike or entry-level mountain bike may no longer be the ideal bike for your riding. When you start to see the speedy commuters and weekend "roadies" pass you on their slick road bikes, and it looks fun to you, it might be time for you to explore road bikes.

The two common styles of road bikes are racing and touring. Both bikes are built for maximum road performance and have many similar features, including general appearance, components, and wheels. Road bikes hug the road and are quick to turn and accelerate. Therefore, road bikes can be too touchy or responsive for novice riders.

Other Styles

There are still many more types of bikes and riding styles. Kids like to do BMX jumps, couples like to ride tandem (on one bike built for two), and families often ride with a baby or small child in tow. Racers ride not only on road and mountain terrain, but they also ride bikes specifically for the types of racing they specialize in. Many folks have started purchasing recumbent bikes or adapting an old bike by taking off gears (making it a single-speed bike), and putting on new handlebars. Others use bikes for delivery purposes, carry large loads on trailers, and run bike taxi services.

Table 2.1 will help you identify and compare bike types, uses, price ranges, and handling. Above all, you need a bike that fits your body and feels comfortable to you while riding. Luckily, there are almost as many types and models of bikes as there are types of riders.

Table 2.1   Bicycle Comparisons

Type of bike	Uses	Price ranges	Handling
Mountain	Off-road, unpaved trails	$400 to $4,000	Rugged
Road (racing)	On-road	$800 to $8,000	Fast, very responsive
Comfort (hybrid)	Around town, paved trails	$250 to $1,000	Easy, comfortable
Touring	On-road, longer distances	$1,000 to $5,000	Sure, solid
Recumbent	On-road, paved trails	$1,000 to $5,000	Varies depending on type
Commuter	Every day	$600 to $1,500	Reliable

FACTORS IN CHOOSING A BIKE

Once you have a feel for the type of bike you are looking for, you must consider a separate set of issues: mainly cost, specific components, and the quality of the materials. Almost any bike sold today will get you from point A to point B; but there are many combinations of components and materials from which to choose, and these are the biggest factors in price.

Cost and Quality

Bicycles are available in a wide range of prices from under $100 up to several thousand dollars. Generally the difference between a $100 bike and a $3,000 bike is the weight, overall quality of the workmanship, components, and frame materials. In addition to the functionality and durability of these elements, their weight and cost are inversely proportional—that is, as the weight goes down, the price goes up. Yet for a minimal investment, you can get a solid bicycle that you can ride for many years with only basic levels of maintenance.

One way to think about the quality–cost consideration is to divide bicycles into four quality categories: low end, entry level, midlevel, and high end.

Low-End Bicycles

Some bicycles are very low end, to the extent that their components are not serviceable, and they have a short life span. Generally, these low-end bikes are found only at big department stores where they lack the skilled technicians and sales staff to help fit the bike properly. These bikes are also often poorly assembled. Many sporting good stores sell low-end bikes, but they may also carry mid- and high-end bikes. Bicycle shops generally do not carry low-end bikes.

Entry-Level Bicycles

Visit most any bike shop, and you will find the full spectrum of entry-level bikes that are intended for long-term use. The key to finding a bike that will last is ensuring that all of its parts are serviceable. Often bikes that have equal frame quality will range widely in price because of the quality of the components, including the **shifters** (the hand controls for a gear shifting system), **drive train** (the parts of a bicycle that have to do with generating forward motion), the front and rear **derailleur** (the mechanism for moving the chain from one sprocket to another to change gears on a multi-speed bicycle), rear **cassette** (a cluster of gears designed for use on a freewheel or rear hub), **crank** (the arm that connects the pedal to the bottom bracket axle), and wheels.

Midlevel Bicycles

Once you are comfortable on a bike, it's often tempting to buy a different bike based on your developing needs. Usually your first bike, often a hybrid bike, is still useful for short distances, but you want to start to ride faster and farther. A midlevel bike has better components, a lighter frame, and smaller tires than many entry-level bikes but still won't set you back more than $800 to $1,000.

High-End Bicycles

Racers and serious cyclists can often be seen with some of the most high-end equipment that costs well into the thousands. Yet high-end bicycles have probably the largest price range. For this discussion, high-end bicycles offer a high-quality frame and components that meet or exceed a user's specific needs. These will be different depending on use and competitive level.

Components

Until you get into the very expensive bikes, the components, or parts, of your bike generally drive the price. Most major bicycle component companies, such as Shimano, Campagnolo, and SRAM, offer a range of components and have a few

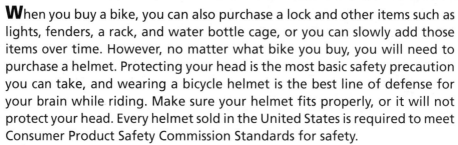

HELMETS ARE VITAL

When you buy a bike, you can also purchase a lock and other items such as lights, fenders, a rack, and water bottle cage, or you can slowly add those items over time. However, no matter what bike you buy, you will need to purchase a helmet. Protecting your head is the most basic safety precaution you can take, and wearing a bicycle helmet is the best line of defense for your brain while riding. Make sure your helmet fits properly, or it will not protect your head. Every helmet sold in the United States is required to meet Consumer Product Safety Commission Standards for safety.

Bicycle helmets are made to last through only one crash—the foam inside compresses to cushion shock to the skull, but it will no longer work after being compressed once. If your helmet is more than five years old or has been dropped on hard ground from a height of more than 4 feet, replace it. New helmets come in a range of sizes with vents and sizing pads for comfort. Make sure to try on a range of helmets to find one that fits and that you will feel comfortable wearing every time you ride.

The helmet should be worn level on your head, with a maximum of two finger widths of forehead showing below your helmet but above your eyebrows. You should be able to see the front of your helmet. It should fit snugly, not moving around on your head even without the straps buckled. Adjust the straps to form a V right under your ears. These straps should be adjusted to prevent the helmet from tilting backward as well. Tighten the chin strap so that no more than one or two fingers fit under the strap. You should be able to open your mouth with the helmet strapped on, but a big yawn should pull the helmet down onto your head. Make adjustments if it rocks forward (obscuring your vision) or slides back toward the back of your head.

Before each ride, check your helmet for damage, and make sure the chin strap is buckled. Don't ride with a helmet that shows cracks or other signs that the foam inside has suffered an impact.

high-end models that differ mostly by weight and small margins of error in performance. It is also possible to buy a frame and add your own selection of components. Beyond that, many frame builders will create a frameset—frame and fork—built to your specifications of size, material, and frame design. This tends to be the most expensive way to acquire a bike, but it will offer the greatest level of customization.

Buy what will serve you. Touring bicycles, for example almost never come with the lightest, most expensive components because they will haul extra weight in racks and bags. High-end mountain bikes can come with either disc or V-brakes, but the advantages of disc brakes will also add to the cost of the bike.

High-end bicycle buyers might seriously consider saving some of their money for a personalized saddle, pedals, shoes, and tires. A $900 touring bike might turn into a $1,200 investment after adding racks and bags. In addition, a top-end saddle (something that every serious cyclist needs), new pedals, and shoes can run into the hundreds. Most bike shops do not allow you to swap these parts at the time of purchase but require that you do your own upgrading. A good shop will do installations for you. Keeping this in mind, it is sometimes better to buy a slightly less expensive bike and better personalized gear for it. To get the most out of any high-end bike, a professional bike fitting goes a long way in saving your knees, back, neck, and hands.

Materials

Bikes come in a variety of materials that serve different needs. People purchasing higher-end bicycles are concerned about the impact of frame material on ride quality, and learning in advance about the differences among materials may affect the quality of your ride.

Steel

Steel and steel alloy bikes have been around for a long time. Steel provides a comfortable, jolt-dampening ride at affordable prices, and steel is strong and easily repaired. Steel is available in a wide variety of dimensions and alloys to suit anything from a superlight hill-climbing bike to a heavy clunker. In addition to weight, ride quality and longevity depend mostly on the quality of the steel tubing. Construction and welding are important, and the steel tubing that makes up the frame can be joined by more methods than any other material.

Aluminum

Aluminum is a light and relatively inexpensive material. Aluminum bikes come with a variety of tube diameters, wall thicknesses, and alloys that all affect the ride quality and longevity. Generally aluminum bikes require larger diameter tubes for strength. As tubes get fatter, the ride will get harsher. Of the frame materials mentioned here, aluminum has the shortest life span. Unlike steel alloys, aluminum doesn't bend. This means that it tends to break, so a crash can lead to serious repair costs.

Titanium

Titanium is a strong and light material known for its resilient, lively ride. Titanium is lighter than steel, but heavier than aluminum. However, these frames are expensive. Titanium is a precious metal, and great care and precision are required in the welding process.

Carbon Fiber

Carbon fiber is very light, strong, and easily tailored to achieve desired strength and stiffness properties. Often used by racers, bikes built with a carbon fiber frame can be fast but have the disadvantage of a higher price tag. Nevertheless, more bikes and components made of carbon fiber are available than ever before. Carbon forks absorb road vibration, so almost every modern racing bike, regardless of the frame material, features a carbon fork. Carbon is the most fragile of the frame materials. Serious surface scratches can lead to long-term cracking of the frame.

BUYING A BIKE

Specialty bike shops or independent bicycle dealers generally carry a wide range of quality products and employ knowledgeable personnel who can help you choose a bike that fits your needs. Specialty shops also provide skilled assembly, fit, and maintenance, which will increase the safety of your bike. You will find that bike shops often specialize; some have a wide selection of mountain bikes while others have commuting gear or perhaps recumbent bicycles. Sporting goods or department stores may also provide a broad selection of bicycles and cycling products and offer useful services.

Bicycles and gear are also available in a variety of Internet and mail-order suppliers. There are clear pros and cons to buying online. We suggest that you purchase your bike at a local dealer so that you can try it out, fit it to yourself, and establish a relationship with the staff of your new bike shop. While buying online can be cheaper and may offer a wider selection, purchasing from a shop allows you to get expert advice and custom fitting. Unlike many products, bikes shouldn't really be tried on in a shop and then purchased online, because so much of the fitting of each bike is personalized after the purchase.

Do Your Research

Before purchasing your bicycle, do some research on the bike market and test ride a variety of bikes. The Internet is a great place to order catalogs, look at different offerings from bike manufacturers, and get advice from cyclists. In addition, bike shops carry catalogs for the brands they stock. While looking at different shops and different types of bikes, test ride as many bikes as you can. Test riding a variety of bikes will help you determine what bike gives you the maximum comfort, handling, and value depending on your needs.

Mix and Match

Many cyclists have a collection of bikes for different uses. A general rule of thumb is that your first bike meets about 75 percent of your needs. Any additional bikes

GETTING BACK IN THE SADDLE

A primary reason that people don't ride bikes is that their bicycle is in disrepair, and they fear it will require a good deal of money to get it fixed. It's always a good idea to try riding before spending a lot of money on any bike. We suggest that you get your bike tuned up, rent a bike every weekend for a month, or borrow a friend's bike to use for a while. That way, when you are ready to buy, you are confident your investment will be worthwhile.

Buying a Bike

Sizing:

- Make sure your child can straddle the top tube with both feet on the ground.
- Adjust the reach of the handlebars so the child is comfortable and sitting upright.
- Bikes should not be "grown into"; buy a bike that safely fits your child.
- Have a bike shop check the fit of your child's bike.

Hand vs. pedal brakes:

- Pedal brakes should be the child's first brakes; teach her to stop at a fixed point.
- Small children may not be able to use hand brakes due to lack of strength and reach.
- Use lever reach adjusters to bring brake levers closer for smaller hands.

Training wheels:

- Start with both training wheels on the ground; gradually move them up every week.
- Children should use training wheels to learn to balance.
- Eventually, raise the training wheels so they don't touch the ground.

BMX:

- Dirt jumping requires safety gear, including full-face helmet, shin pads, and gloves.
- Beginners should also consider elbow pads, knee pads, and wrist guards.
- Not all bikes are strong enough to jump; check with your local bike shop.

Freestyle:

- Flatland trick riding requires safety gear; helmet, gloves, and shin pads are important.
- Freestyle bikes have pegs on the front and rear axles that allow standing.
- Never allow your child to transport other children on her bike.

Mountain:

- Children should wear a helmet and gloves when mountain biking.
- Ride or walk with your child to become familiar with the trails.
- Set specific boundaries for where your child can and cannot ride.

specialize for specific uses. For example, a commuter bike might meet most of your needs, but if you are planning a trip across the country you might purchase a touring bike. A second example would be a racing bike—if you are a regular commuter, but you want to see faster times on your weekend rides, investing in a road bike will help shave off the minutes. While some think they need the perfect machine for each ride, it is also possible to mix and match parts and accessories to make a single bike practical for any of its potential uses. For example, a mountain bike with a set of narrow slick tires can be ridden on the road to achieve a ride similar to that of a road bike.

Achieve Proper Fit

Your bike should fit your body for reasons of safety, comfort, and efficiency. If you are buying a new bicycle, take the opportunity to make sure it fits you properly. The frame of the bicycle is the key to proper fit. You should have adequate clearance between you and the top tube when standing over the bike with both feet flat on the ground. With a road bike you want 1 to 2 inches of clearance between you and the top tube. For a mountain or hybrid bike, there should be 3 to 4 inches (figure 2.7). Because mountain bike riding tends to take place on rugged, uneven terrain, cyclists need to be able to get on and off the bike quickly—the additional clearance helps with this.

Frame size is typically measured from the bottom bracket's center to the center or top of the top tube where it joins the seat tube. Frame size is usually measured in centimeters for road bicycles, and in inches for hybrid and mountain bikes. Some mountain bikes simply come in small, medium, large, and extra large. Typically, you should pick a mountain bike that is 4 to 5 inches smaller than you require in a road frame. Once you have a frame that is the proper size, you or your retailer can make a few minor adjustments to improve your cycling experience.

- *Saddle height.* Sitting on the saddle with the ball of the foot on the pedal, you need a slight bend in the knee when the pedal is at the very bottom of the pedal stroke (ideally 30 degrees) (figure 2.8). If your hips rock when pedaling, the seat is too high. If your hips bounce, the seat is too low.

- *Seat angle.* The nose of the saddle should be level with the rear of the saddle, and the saddle should be parallel to the ground.

- *Seat position.* The forward–aft position of the saddle should be adjusted so that the front of your forward knee is directly above the center of the pedal when you have both pedals parallel to the ground. Some seat post designs can be set back more than others, further adjusting your position relative to the pedals. A few millimeters can make a difference.

- *Stem length and angle.* The **stem** connects your bike frame to the handlebars. If you experience discomfort in your back or shoulders, ask your retailer about switching to a longer or shorter stem. A more upright stem will allow you to sit more upright, while a lower rise (less upright angle) permits a more aerodynamic position.

- *Handlebars.* Handlebar angle and height should be adjusted for rider comfort.

- *Brake lever position.* The brake lever should be adjusted so that you can comfortably reach and apply the brakes. You should seek to achieve a straight line through your arms, wrists, hands, and fingers.

a

b

Figure 2.7 *(a)* A road bike needs to have 1 to 2 inches of clearance when you are standing over the top tube; *(b)* a mountain bike needs 3 to 4 inches. These are crude measurements that will be refined by a good bike shop, but they do serve as a good rule of thumb.

Figure 2.8 When your leg is fully extended on the pedal, your knee should have just a slight bend, as shown.

If you haven't been riding regularly, it will take some time before your muscles adjust to this new exercise position. Your legs, posterior, back, hands, and neck may be a bit sore for a few days after your first long bike ride. If there are any sharp pains, or your symptoms last more than a week, check with a bike shop representative or your physician. Your bicycle retailer may be able to alleviate these problems by adjusting your position on the bike.

CONCLUSION

Learning what style of riding you like best and what bike fits that style, and then buying a bike that matches you, is a fun part of being and becoming a cyclist. Whether you choose a low-end hybrid or a recumbent tricycle with a fairing added for speed, bicycling is a great way to get around town.

RULES OF THE **ROAD**

Each type of cycling generally has its own etiquette or rules of the road. Bicycle racers and users of paths, trails, and roads all have to follow their own rules and protocols. But when bicyclists use the public roads and right of way, they have a special code to follow: the vehicle code.

In all 50 states, bicyclists are classified as operators of vehicles. And like any vehicle operator that is using the public right of way, you need to know a complex set of traffic rules and regulations to function safely and predictably. In addition to understanding and following the basic rules of the road, bicyclists must learn user principles that will help guide them to safe road use and positioning.

The league's Smart Cycling program teaches bicyclists to ride their bikes like vehicles. Specifically, the Smart Cycling program promotes a set of rules and concepts for bicyclists to follow when cycling on the road. These concepts cover where to be and how to behave on the road.

And yes, as a cyclist, you should plan to ride on the road. Sidewalks are built for the speed and size of pedestrians, not cyclists. If you hope to get anywhere on a bicycle, the road is your friend. Luckily there are many roads, many road types, and many choices you can make about where to ride in your community. You will also learn which roads work best for you, or perhaps you will discover that your community needs better streets for cycling, and you will work to help make that happen.

This chapter presents the basic legal concepts for cycling and the principles to follow to increase safety. Because all states have different vehicle codes, this chapter addresses the laws as generally laid out in many states, not the laws of every state. Look to your state's bicycle coordinator for information, or refer to the state department of motor vehicles for the laws that pertain to you in a certain state. Local jurisdictions may also have their own slightly different vehicle codes to follow.

DRIVING YOUR BIKE

For many people, the bike is their primary form of transportation. Most regular cyclists understand the principles of cycling and apply them at every turn to be safe. That is, they drive their bike as if it were a vehicle. In fact, studies by the Federal Highway Administration (1995) show that obeying the rules of the road and driving your bike as if it were a vehicle dramatically increase bicyclists' safety and reduce crash rates. So while cycling is not without its risks, your risks are drastically reduced if you master these basic principles. Safe riders are attuned to road conditions and the traffic laws as they apply to bicycles. As you learn the principles

THREE SIMPLE WAYS TO REDUCE YOUR RISK OF CRASHING

1. Ride in the street.
2. Ride in the direction of traffic.
3. Stop and yield at signs and intersections.

Source: walkinginfo.org: Pedestrian and Bicycle Information Center, n.d.

outlined in this book, you will also improve your ability to handle your bike and avoid hazardous situations.

The bicycle is a vehicle and has all of the same rights and responsibilities as other vehicles. Therefore, bicyclists must follow all traffic signals and signs, ride on the right with traffic, and remain predictable. However, bicyclists have some additional laws to follow, such as giving an audible signal when passing pedestrians, and cyclists are granted certain freedoms, such as riding in bike lanes. Bicyclists may travel two abreast in a traffic lane in most states, but some states require bicyclists to travel in single file in certain locations or under certain conditions. Bicyclists also have to obey laws about using sidewalks, multiuse paths, helmets, lights, and other equipment. Clearly, it is a good idea to check the local vehicle code for your state. The league's Web site, at www.bikeleague.org, has links to vehicle codes pertaining to bicycles in all 50 states.

The vehicle code is fairly complex, but if you drive a car, you should already have a firm understanding of it. And as it is generally applied, the principles are fairly straightforward. The key concept of the vehicle code is predictability; traffic laws help ensure that all vehicle users can predict what other operators will do. These principles are used at every turn and are the basis for determination of fault when collisions occur.

Applying the traffic principles requires facility in bike handling, mounting and dismounting, and scanning and signaling. As you gain experience with increasingly complex traffic situations, you will gain confidence and have greater success with applying these principles. As with any new skill, your first rides in traffic may be challenging, but they should not be harrowing. The more experience and skill you develop, the more comfortable you will feel.

First Come, First Served

A driver on the road is entitled to the space the vehicle is using, with reasonable clearance on all sides and reasonable stopping distance in front. Drivers who wish to use this space must yield to the vehicle already using it.

Traveling on the Right

By traveling on the right-hand side of the roadway, you are behaving in a predictable manner. From this position, you can readily function as part of the traffic flow and make sure the actions of motorists do not put you in jeopardy (figure 3.1).

It is important to learn how far to the right you should travel. Traffic laws in many jurisdictions direct bicyclists to ride as far to the right as is practicable. The law says "practicable," not "possible," so you do not have to ride in the gutter and dodge drain grates, glass, and gravel. It means you should ride far enough to the right to allow traffic to pass—provided this is safe for you. It also means you have a right to travel far enough away from parked cars, the curb, or the edge of the road to avoid hazards and increase your visibility to motorists.

Yielding to Cross Traffic

A driver entering a roadway from a driveway, alley, or smaller or less used road must stop and yield the right of way to traffic on the main roadway. Yielding means proceeding onto a roadway only when it is safe to do so.

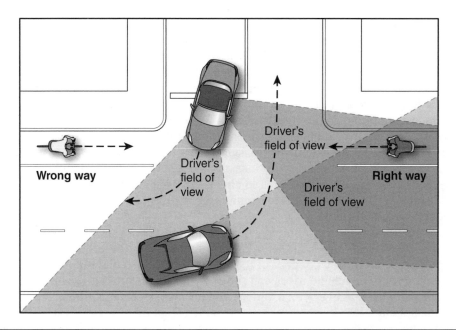

Figure 3.1 Drivers of vehicles, including bicyclists, must drive on the right-hand side of the roadway. Traveling against traffic puts you in positions on the road where other drivers do not expect you to be and makes it impossible for you to read signs and signals.

Changing Lanes

Changing lanes in traffic is most frequently done when a bicyclist is attempting to make a left turn and must reposition himself from the right side to the center of the street. He may also need to change lanes to avoid hazards or stopped vehicles, for merging lanes, or to adjust for speed positioning (overtake slower-moving vehicles).

A driver who wishes to change lanes must yield to traffic in the new lane. For cyclists, this requires a maneuver called scanning. Scanning refers to looking over your shoulder to check for traffic, making eye contact and communicating with motorists and others and looking for other hazards such as dogs or debris, cracks in the pavement, or slippery metal grates. Scanning also serves as a signal to motorists; they see your head turn and note that you probably intend to change lanes (figure 3.2).

To change lanes in traffic, you must do the following:

1. Plan ahead; leave time to position yourself.

2. Look behind you by scanning over your shoulder, perhaps several times.

3. Be aware of overtaking vehicles and your speed relative to the speed of other vehicles.

4. Use signals, eye contact, and body language to make others aware of your intention and gain their cooperation.

5. Change lanes gradually, moving twice per lane (from the right to the left side of each lane), scanning and signaling, repeating these steps to move laterally from lane to lane. Keep your speed as close as possible to that of the traffic around you.

Figure 3.2 Making eye contact with drivers is one of the easiest ways to let them know your intentions and interact with them safely.

6. Never create a hazardous situation by cutting too close in front of a moving vehicle.

Act carefully, smoothly, and deliberately but confidently. Ride in a straight and steady line in your final riding position. Motorists respond respectfully when you appear to know what you're doing.

Signaling

A large part of being predictable in your actions on the highway is letting others know what you plan to do before you do it—hand signals are a vital communication tool. Scanning behind you while riding in traffic may act as a secondary signal to motorists that you plan to change your position on the roadway. Signals help other vehicle operators know what you intend, but just because you signal doesn't mean it is safe to turn. Use your judgment, and if you feel it is too dangerous, pull over to the side and let traffic clear before you complete your maneuver.

Figure 3.3 shows signals for a left turn, a right turn, and a stop.

- A left turn is signaled with the left arm straight out to the side as if you are pointing left.

- A right turn is made with the left arm bent upward at the elbow, or with the right hand pointed straight out to the right side. The right-turn signal has historically been the left arm outstretched and bent upward at the elbow, but since this signal may be difficult for motorists to see, some states now allow the right outstretched arm to indicate a right turn.

- A stop is made with the left arm bent downward at the elbow.

a

b

c

d

Figure 3.3 When you are comfortable on your bike, hand gestures are another good way to signal your intentions to drivers. There are signals for *(a)* left turns, *(b* and *c)* two options for right turns, and *(d)* a signal to stop.

Always use hand signals when turning, when changing lanes, and even when changing position in a given lane. Motorists will appreciate the courtesy and respond in kind. In addition, be sure to stop signaling well before entering the intersection. At this point, it is more important for you to have both hands on the handlebar for maximum control and maneuverability.

Speed Positioning

As a cyclist, you are entitled to a position in the traffic flow. While classified and functioning as a vehicle, a bike is significantly different than a car, and that poses some particular challenges. The slower the vehicle is traveling, the farther right it should be in the roadway. For example, cars park by the curb, slow-moving cars travel to the left of parked cars, and the next lane to the left is for faster-moving traffic. This rule promotes smooth traffic flow. Bikes should not overtake another vehicle on the right. Exceptions to this rule include when the vehicle ahead is turning left, or when traveling on multilane roads or in a bike lane. In slow, downtown traffic, you will be faster than many of the cars, so position yourself according to your relative speed (figure 3.4).

Because bicycles are narrow vehicles, it is often possible to share a traffic lane with a motor vehicle. When the lane is wide enough to share, ride just to the right (3 or 4 feet) of the motorized traffic. If the lane is too narrow for you to safely share, ride in the center to fully occupy the lane. (This is referred to as taking the lane.) Motorists who want to pass you will be unable to squeeze past and remain in the lane. They will have to acknowledge that they are passing another vehicle, wait for oncoming traffic to clear, and pull across the centerline or over into the lane to the left of yours.

When you are traveling at about the same speed, you are in the flow of traffic and should ride in the middle of the lane. In the center of the lane you are more visible to cars entering the roadway or turning left. You need the extra space around you for safety at high speed.

If you are moving slower than the traffic around you—for example, if you are grinding up a hill at a slow speed—move to the right. When riding slowly, it is possible to ride safely within a foot of the edge of the road, but generally, you want to avoid the area close to the curb (where debris accumulates and cars may be parked) and ride closer to the middle of the road. Pick a good line and stay straight on it to be predictable to other drivers. Do not allow your path to swerve.

In a very wide lane (14 feet or greater), there may be room for you to ride several feet from the curb and still allow traffic to pass on your left. In this situation, it is safer to ride just to the right (3 or 4 feet) of faster traffic. You are more visible; you can avoid car doors opening into you; you can be seen by vehicles entering the roadway; and you will reduce the hazard to you from road debris that collects near the curb. You are not delaying traffic in that position, and it is the safest place for you to travel.

Rural roads can present a particular challenge where lanes are narrow and speeds are high. You will need to be concerned generally about being visible to motorists. When passing over the crest of a hill, ride as far to the right as possible. You still have a right to your position in the lane, but you may face an added challenge of an overtaking car heading toward you in your lane. In such a situation, where the passing car going in the opposite direction as you may be traveling too fast to react to your presence, it is advisable to look for a place to pull off the road until the driver is safely past you.

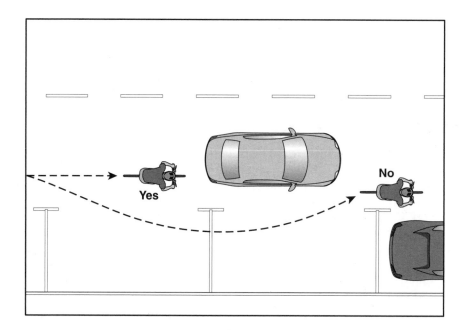

Figure 3.4 If traveling at the speed of traffic, a bicyclist should control the lane unless it is a very wide lane. If traveling faster than other traffic, overtake on the left, keeping a safe distance from slower traffic.

Intersections

Approach intersections in the proper position. Vehicles turning right are closest to the curb, those turning left are near the centerline, and straight-through drivers are between these positions. Always travel in the right-most lane that leads to your destination. In single-destination lanes (or a two-lane street), ride on the right-hand side of the lane, except when stopping at a light when you plan to proceed straight through or when preparing for a left-hand turn.

Stopping at a Light

As you approach the intersection at a red light, give yourself plenty of time to scan behind you and look at the driver behind you, then signal, indicating that you are taking the lane. If the driver fails to yield, you can wait and simply stop behind the vehicle instead.

If you're turning right, stay toward the right of the lane to indicate to the motorists behind you that you plan to turn at the light. However, if you plan to move straight through the intersection, position yourself in the middle of the lane. The danger of being to the right side when you are proceeding straight through is that motorists will pass and cut you off by turning right around you. If you position yourself in the center of the lane—by waiting behind the other waiting vehicles or standing astride your bike in the middle of the lane at the light—you'll let cars know you're proceeding straight, and you'll be more visible. As the light changes, you can gradually move over when it's safe to do so (check for parked cars on the right) and allow the other vehicles to pass you.

Turning Left

Left turns can be taken as a pedestrian would, by dismounting on the right side of the road and walking the bike across at controlled intersections. They can also be done more smoothly and swiftly by turning like a vehicle in traffic. Execute these turns only where you feel comfortable and after having practiced in low-traffic situations.

When preparing for a left-hand turn, you must move from the right lane to the right side of the left-turn lane farthest to the right. To get there, scan over your left shoulder, signal your move, and move twice per lane. In heavy traffic, you may be negotiating with drivers who want to pass. Make it clear what you are doing, remember you have the right to make a left turn from the same lane from which the cars are turning, and make sure you're visible to drivers. On a two-lane street with no dedicated left-turn lane, you will simply move to the left side of the traffic lane moving in your direction, signal your turn, and yield to oncoming traffic.

To turn left on multiple-lane streets, you will have to cross over into the left lane or dedicated left-turn lane. If you are stopped for a light in this lane, position yourself according to the size of the lane. If it's wide enough to share with a car, you can stay to the right of the lane. If it's too narrow for both you and a car to comfortably share, take the lane. As a cyclist, you should be in the same lane you would be in if you were driving a car. Your position in the lane is an effective signal to other drivers to let them know which way you are going (figure 3.5). If there are double left-turn lanes, stay in the right-most one.

When executing the left turn, arc smoothly through to arrive at the right-hand side of the lane going in your direction. If you're moving at the speed of traffic, take

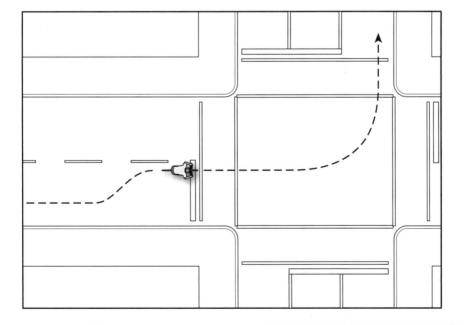

Figure 3.5 When you need to change multiple lanes and traffic is heavy and moving about your speed, negotiate with overtaking motorists by scanning and signaling.

and hold the lane through the turn. Check for cars turning right on red that might be entering the same lane as you. You should yield to them.

Riding in Bike Lanes

On a roadway with bike lanes, you should treat the bike lane as an extra lane for cyclists only (that is, a lane that cars are not meant to use) and follow the rule of riding in the right-most lane that goes to your destination (figure 3.6). If the bike lane has debris or parked cars or is otherwise hazardous, you are not legally obliged to use it.

Never make a left-hand turn directly from a bike lane unless it is one specifically designed for bikes turning left. To make a left-hand turn at an upcoming intersection, you will need to get to the center of the street or regular left-turn lane by making your two lateral moves per lane. You must begin the process of changing lanes well before the turn.

Bike lanes provide many benefits for cyclists. Generally, because bike lanes are dedicated for cyclists, cyclists have elevated rights when traveling in them. For example, autos are not allowed to park in or impede the flow of a bicyclist in a bike lane. Bicyclists in a bike lane are also generally allowed to pass cars on the right, when they normally cannot do this. However, even though a cyclist has the right of way when going straight through an intersection, riders must be aware of right-turning vehicles that could cut them off. In a no-bike-lane situation, the auto has the right of way because bikers cannot pass a car on the right. In the bike lane, cyclists may have the right of way but should still be cautious; they will always lose in the event of a collision.

Well-placed and well-designed bike lanes are safe and fun to use. Bike lanes and other bicycle-friendly infrastructures have been shown to increase bicycling use,

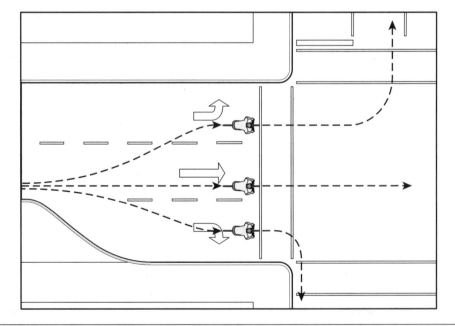

Figure 3.6 Generally speaking, as a bicyclist, you should be in the right-most lane that goes in the direction you are traveling.

and with increased use and visibility, bicycling becomes safer and more visible to motorists.

However, bike lanes may also be poorly placed and designed. Cyclists should watch out for these situations and consider leaving the bike lane if it is in an awkward location. Sometimes bike lanes are on busy streets, and there may be a safer, more enjoyable route to your destination. In addition, bike lanes may have debris and other problems that might lead you to edge out of it or ride in the traffic lane. Ultimately, you should choose how you use or don't use bike lanes, so remember to follow your instincts and the traffic principles.

Riding on Multiuse Paths and Trails

Many bicyclists enjoy riding on multiuse paths. A multiuse path is an off-road facility, generally paved, that accommodates bicycles, pedestrians, and other nonmotorized users. Multiuse or shared-use paths are growing in popularity and numbers, and they often provide pleasant transportation connections for bicyclists. Multiuse paths are often called trails and may have been built over an abandoned railroad path or along a river. They generally do not follow a street, as a sidewalk does, and they are wider than sidewalks to accommodate different users.

SHARING PATHS AND TRAILS

Recreational paths and trails can be very congested, making safety an issue. Whether bicycling, walking, or jogging, following the same rules as everyone else will help you have a safer, more enjoyable time.

Bicyclists must always yield to pedestrians on multiuse paths and sidewalks, and the speed-positioning rule applies. Most important, bicyclists must provide an audible signal when passing pedestrians and other cyclists. Bicyclists should also consider slowing down a bit on these paths as there are many types of users.

Trails have engineering and design limitations that require you to ride differently than you would on the road. If your preferred speed or style of cycling is inappropriate for trails, look for better-suited alternative routes. Riding trails with friends or family can be quite enjoyable if you obey the rules of the trail (figure 3.7).

Be Courteous

All trail users should be respectful of other users, regardless of their mode of travel, speed, or skill level. Modify your speed when interacting with other trail users to ensure everyone's safety.

Never ride directly behind someone going close to your speed (called **pacelining**) unless you have permission. Some other fast-moving trail users, including other cyclists and in-line skaters, may not know this etiquette and may paceline behind you. Simply wave them by, or slow down, indicating that you are not comfortable with their proximity.

Respect the Right of Way

Know the rules on right of way on the trail you're using. Trails may have local variations of the standard roadway rules. If you don't know your local rules, a good rule

Figure 3.7 Riding on multiuse paths can be a lovely way to spend an afternoon. It is important to understand that you must always yield to slower trail users, though, and be especially cautious around children and pets.

of thumb is that cyclists should yield to all other trail users. Most trails post signs signaling who yields to whom, and almost all trails expect you to ride on the right and pass on the left. Practice special caution when interacting with horses, dogs, or small children.

Give an Audible Signal When Passing

Warn in advance those whom you are passing so that you have time to maneuver if necessary. This signal may be a bell, horn, or voice. Loudly and clearly saying, "Passing on your left," is the most common signal used to alert other users of your approach. If you think a group or a trail user (possibly wearing headphones) has not heard you, be especially cautious when passing. Repeat, "Passing on your left," as you approach, and be ready to stop quickly if they are startled into your path by your passing.

When others notify you that they are passing you, it is courteous to slow down and move to the right to give them room to pass. If you feel they are passing you unsafely, it is best to slow or stop and allow them to pass.

Pass on the Left

Pass others who are going in your direction on their left. Look ahead and behind to make sure the lane is clear before pulling out. Do not move back to the right until safely past. Fast-moving users, like cyclists, are responsible for yielding to slower-moving users. When passing people, make sure you have enough room to get safely back on your side of the trail before encountering oncoming trail users. If you don't have plenty of room, slow down and wait before passing. Never try to pass without plenty of room—it's dangerous and rude, and slowing down to let oncoming traffic pass takes only a few seconds.

Yield When Entering and Crossing Other Trails

When entering or crossing a trail at trail intersections, yield to traffic on the cross trail or road. This is often the most dangerous point on a trail. Intersections are a very common place for crashes to occur, often because everyone assumes the right of way. To be a safe cyclist, assume you *do not* have the right of way. Stop and look both ways before proceeding, and ride or walk your bike quickly across the intersection.

Be Predictable

Ride in a straight line. Warn other trail users of your intentions by indicating when you are turning, slowing, or stopping.

Use Lights at Night

If the trail is open and you are using it between dusk and dawn, you must be equipped with lights. Bikes need a white front light and a red rear light or reflector. Reflectors and reflective clothing are no help if there is no source of light.

Clean Up Litter

Do not leave any debris along the trail. If you have trash, carry it until you find a trash can. Go the extra step—pack out more trash than you bring in.

RIDING ON SIDEWALKS AND IN CROSSWALKS

Riding on sidewalks is generally not advised and is illegal in some areas. Sidewalks are not designed for the pace of bicycles and therefore are not safe for such use. For example, according to the American Association of State Highway and Transportation Officials (1999), pedestrians exiting stores or cars crossing the sidewalk on driveways can present hazards for bicyclists. Fixed objects such as parking meters, utility poles, sign posts, bus benches, trees, fire hydrants, and mail boxes can make sidewalks an obstacle course. Walkers, joggers, skateboarders, and roller skaters change their speed and direction unpredictably, leaving bicyclists with insufficient reaction time to avoid collisions.

In general, riding on the sidewalk changes the classification of a bicycle from a vehicle to a pedestrian. Therefore, cyclists must follow a different set of rules on sidewalks and are often restricted in riding speeds.

In many states, the general rule is that cyclists can ride freely on sidewalks but should ride at pedestrian speed at intersections, crosswalks, curbcuts, and driveways when cars are present. Because pedestrian speed is 2 to 3 miles per hour, you may as well be walking your bike. Bicyclists who ride their bike off sidewalks into

CHILDREN AND SIDEWALKS

The key thing to remember about sidewalks is that they aren't designed for fast cyclists. For young children learning to ride and even for older children who have mastered the skills of riding but are not yet ready to ride in busy traffic, sidewalks are perfectly legitimate places to ride and may well be the safer option. However, that's only true if they know to stop when they get to an intersection or slow and yield at driveways; to yield to pedestrians and other users on the sidewalk; and to ride at a reasonable speed.

intersections at higher speeds are generally not visible to motorists, are not being predictable, and are at much greater danger of being hit by a turning motorist. In this instance, the cyclist will probably bear the liability of an accident.

In the few locations where riding on a sidewalk might make sense, cyclists must yield to pedestrians. Cyclists must give an audible signal when passing pedestrians and maintain a safe distance from pedestrians.

RIDING WITH A GROUP

If you are riding in a group, there are some group riding rules to follow. You are responsible for your own safety when riding in a group (figure 3.8). If you are planning on riding in a major ride with more than 100 riders, be sure to take the league's course Group Riding Skills. To sign up, visit the league's Web site at www.bikeleague.org, then click on Find It to find a class in your area.

When riding in a group, use no more than half the width of the trail. On many heavy-use trails, this means that all users will need to stay single file. If you stop to regroup, always do it off the trail.

Be Predictable

Group riding requires even more attention to predictability than riding alone. Other riders will expect you to continue riding at a constant speed and lane position, following the road or trail, unless you indicate differently.

Use Signals

Use hand and verbal signals to communicate with others in the group and with motorists. Hand signals, except for the standard hand signals, may vary by region, so make sure you know and agree to the same set of signals.

Give Warnings

Warn cyclists behind you of changes in direction or speed. The lead rider should call, "Left," or "Right," in addition to using a hand signal. The lead rider should announce the turn well in advance of the intersection so members of the group have time to position themselves and can turn without conflict.

Figure 3.8 Riding in a group helps you go faster and adds enjoyment to your ride. Be sure to be courteous of other riders!

Change Positions Correctly

You should pass others on their left. Say, "On your left," to warn others that you are passing. If you need to pass someone on the right, say, "On your right," clearly and be careful since this is an unusual maneuver.

Announce Hazards

Most of the cyclists riding in a group will not have a good view of the road surface ahead, so it is important to announce hazards. Indicate hazards by pointing down to the left or right and shouting, "Hole," or "Bump." Everyone should be made aware of hazards; however, everyone does not need to announce them.

Watch for Traffic Coming From the Rear

Even when you are occupying the proper lane position, it often helps to know when a car is coming. Since those in front cannot see traffic approaching from the rear, it is the responsibility of the riders in back to inform the others by saying, "Car back." Around curves, on narrow roads, or when riding double, it is also helpful to warn of traffic approaching from ahead with "Car up."

Be Careful at Intersections

When approaching intersections that require vehicles to yield or stop, the lead rider should say, "Slowing," or "Stopping," to alert those behind. When passing through an intersection, some bicyclists say, "Clear," if there is no cross traffic. This is a dangerous practice and should not be followed. It encourages riders to let others do their thinking for them. Each bicyclist is responsible for his own safety.

Leave a Gap for Cars

When riding up hills or on narrow roads, leave a gap between every three or four bicyclists so motorists can pass smaller groups. This is not only courteous but also safer. Motorists will not get frustrated and try to pass when other traffic is approaching. You can signal drivers when it is unsafe to pass, but for liability reasons you probably shouldn't take on the responsibility of waving someone past when you see the road is clear.

Move off the Road to Stop

When the group stops, move well off the road so you do not interfere with traffic. When you start again, each bicyclist should look for and yield to traffic.

Riding Single File or Two Abreast

Ride single file or two abreast as appropriate to the roadway and traffic conditions, as allowed by law. Most state vehicle codes permit narrow vehicles such as bicycles and motorcycles to ride two abreast within the lane. Even where riding double is legal, courtesy dictates that you ride single file when cars are trying to pass you if the lane is wide enough for them to safely do so. Riding more than two abreast is almost always illegal unless the road is closed to motorized traffic.

TIPS FOR MOTORISTS

About 98 million people in the United States own bicycles, according to the National Bicycle Dealers Association (2009). According to the National Highway Traffic Safety Administration (2008), about 700 bicyclists are killed each year in the United States, and NHTSA also shows that approximately 96 percent of these deaths result from crashes with motor vehicles. In all 50 states, bicyclists are expected to obey the same laws as drivers of motor vehicles, but they are also accorded the same rights. Don't be the cause of a crash between a vehicle and a bicycle. Follow these guidelines when driving around cyclists.

- Leave at least three feet of passing space between the right side of your vehicle and a bicyclist.
- Be aware that when a road is too narrow for cars and bikes to ride safely side by side, it is safest for bicyclists to take the travel lane, which means riding in or near the center of the lane. This is allowed in the laws of all 50 states.
- Reduce your speed when passing a cyclist, especially if the roadway is narrow.
- When turning left at an intersection, yield to an oncoming bicyclist just as you would yield to an oncoming motorist.
- After passing a cyclist on your right, check over your shoulder to make sure you have allowed adequate distance before merging back in.

Kid's-Eye View

Rules of the Road

When children start to ride their bicycles, they need to understand that bikes are vehicles; this is their first introduction to driver's training. Be sure to ride with them on their first few big trips; plan a route with your child to get him to a friend's house or school by bike. Around age 10, children are ready for longer trips—be sure you have ridden with them enough to trust they will make safe decisions on their bikes.

- Don't honk your horn when approaching bicyclists.
- In inclement weather, give cyclists extra room, just as you would other motorists.
- Look for approaching situations and obstacles that may be hazardous to cyclists, such as potholes, debris, and glass, and then give them adequate space to maneuver.
- Look for bicyclists before opening your car door on the traffic side.
- Children on bicycles often act unpredictably: Expect the unexpected.

CONCLUSION

If you had to boil all the rules of the road down to just one sentence, it would be this: Drive your bike as you would your car. If you stop at stop signs, ride only on the correct side of the street or trail, and are courteous to other users around you, you're well on your way to being an excellent cyclist.

BICYCLE HANDLING SKILLS

In addition to following the rules of the road and road position rules, you can increase your safety by learning how to handle your bicycle skillfully. These skills begin with your general knowledge of your bike and its ability to accelerate, corner, and stop. Next, you should learn to ride with one hand on the handlebars, scan over either shoulder for traffic, and be visible on the street. Finally, you should also acquire a specific set of skills to avoid hazards and handle emergency situations that are useful for any regular cyclist.

GETTING TO KNOW YOUR BICYCLE

All bicycles are different and have different rides, feels, and abilities to perform different functions. Does your bike have weak or strong brakes? Do your tires slip on wet pavement or do they corner well in all conditions? How about your ability to accelerate? Is it time to take your bike to the shop for regular or specific maintenance repairs because it performs so poorly? All of these factors should play into your riding strategy and style.

A safe cyclist will use her bike within the limits of the bike's intended use, such as whether the bike can take a corner fast or should the rider slow down and enjoy the cruise. Once you are comfortable on your bicycle and know its abilities, you can use it to its full potential (figure 4.1).

Figure 4.1 Testing your bike lean capabilities will help you become familiar with your bicycle.

BASIC RIDING MANEUVERS

Every bicyclist should understand the basic skills and techniques required for effectively operating a bike. Once you know how to ride confidently, it all seems like second nature. Before that, though, even getting on your bike can be a bit of a challenge. The next few sections walk you through mounting, starting, stopping, turning, and changing gears—the key things you need to know to ride your bike with confidence and skill.

Mounting, Starting, and Stopping

Before riding, you have to master getting on your bike. To mount the bike, lift one leg over the frame while tipping the bike about 45 degrees toward you. As you step over, hold the handlebars, and right the bike again so that you end up standing over the top tube. Squeeze both brakes to steady the bike. Using either foot, rotate the crank backward until a pedal is at the two o'clock position on the face of a clock—forward and high.

To get started, stand on one foot and place the other foot on the pedal at the two o'clock position. Release the brakes and push down on the pedal, allowing your body to lift up onto the saddle. Sit on the saddle, put both feet on the pedals, and start pedaling. If you are a beginner and you feel unstable as you put a foot on the pedal and slide onto the seat, it may help to lower your seat several inches. After you feel more stable, readjust your seat back to the proper height.

Braking is a critical skill. Hand brakes are the most common brakes on adult bikes. Generally the right-hand lever controls the rear brake; the left-hand lever controls the front brake. Gradually apply both brakes together to produce a smooth, steady deceleration, with slightly more pressure on the front one. Just as you come to a complete stop, turn the handlebars a little bit away from the side you want to step down on. The bike will lean to that side so you can step down.

The front brake has considerably more stopping power than the rear when the bicycle is moving forward. To capitalize on this greater stopping power, the general rule is to use both brakes but to apply more pressure to the front brake (*up to three times more in an emergency*) than the rear. In fact, the front brake is so powerful that it should be used only in conjunction with the rear brake. Improper application of the front brake can pitch the bike over the front wheel and send you over the front of the bike. Also avoid using only the rear brake. The rear brake will not stop you quickly; use both brakes to stop effectively and quickly.

Mounting, starting, and stopping your bike are the first skills you must feel confident doing. If you cannot mount, start, and stop quickly and safely, you put yourself and others at risk. Master these skills by practicing in a traffic-free environment. Find an empty parking lot or some other open space where you can practice and gain confidence in your bike-handling ability.

Turning

It is important that your bicycle turn in the direction you desire, and doing this is as much about weight distribution as it is about steering. When you approach a right turn, for example, you actually turn your bike to the left a tiny bit (it is instinctive, not something you need to think about). This helps shift your weight into the turn.

The tighter the turn is, the stronger the lean. In a great, swooping turn, with lots of room around you, the lean is imperceptible. Even on a tight turn it's hard to see but important to understand: In addition to steering your bike, your weight distribution is what makes a turn successful.

Intuitively you might believe that your hands on the handlebars steer the bike, but it is possible to steer your bike when riding without hands. In fact, leaning to change weight distribution is what truly turns your bike. This is why a rider must lean into sharp turns. Turning on a bicycle is more easily practiced than explained!

Using Gears

One of the reasons the bicycle is the most efficient means of transportation is the gearing (figure 4.2). Bikes today are available with as many as 11 cogs in the rear, making up a cassette, and three chainrings up front, giving the cyclist a wide range of gears with small variations between gears. **Cog** and **chainring** are terms for the toothed sprockets that your chain hooks into and turn the wheels when pedaled. The *cassette* is the term for the group of cogs on your rear gears. Understanding how gears work and when and how to shift between them will allow you to adjust for variations in speed and terrain.

Whether you use them all or not, you have many gears on your bike enabling you to exert nearly the same amount of pedaling effort whether you're riding up a hill, down a hill, or on level ground at a wide range of speeds.

For good efficiency and low impact on your knees, most people find a pedaling **cadence** (the rate of rotation of the pedals) of 75 to 95 **rpm** (revolutions per minute) to work for them. You can determine your cadence by counting how many times one pedal goes around in a minute.

Cassette with cogs (gears are what you switch, involving chainrings and cogs)

Chainrings

Figure 4.2　The cogs, chainrings, and cassette all help you ride in a variety of settings, from flat roads to hilly terrain.

When you are maintaining a steady cadence, the bike will travel different distances depending on the gear you select. For example, when a bike is in high gear, each revolution of the pedals propels it a long distance—perhaps 30 feet or so—but pedaling effort is very high. When the bike is in low gear, each revolution propels it only a short distance—perhaps as little as 10 feet—but the pedals are easier to turn.

On modern bikes, you have fingertip access to both the front and the rear derailleurs. Bikes may have down-tube shifters (mounted on the diagonal tube on older style road bikes), shift levers that are integrated with the brake lever (on newer road bikes), or twist or trigger-style shifters (on mountain bikes, hybrids, or any bike with a flat bar), among others. Generally, your left shifter moves the front derailleur, which moves the chain from one chainring to another when pedaling. The right shifter operates the rear derailleur, moving the chain from one rear cog to another.

If your bike has three chainrings, you will do much of your riding in the middle one. Most of your shifting, then, will be done with your right hand, using the rear derailleur to find a comfortable gear. Derailleurs are the transmission system of your bicycle, moving the chain up and down the gears. When using the derailleurs, you should remember to shift only when pedaling.

If the change in terrain is pronounced, you will need to shift the front derailleur as well. Move it onto a smaller chainring (toward the bike) for a lower gear (for instance, when climbing a hill) and onto a larger chainring (away from the bike) for a higher gear. While pedaling, use the shifter at your left hand to move the chain. Remember, moving the chain toward the bike makes it easier to pedal, and moving the chain away from the bike makes it harder to pedal.

Shifting the Front Derailleur

Using your left hand to shift the left gear lever moves the chain from one front chainring to another and can have a dramatic effect on the force it takes to pedal your bike. You will likely have two or three chainrings. Think of them as high (big ring) and low (small ring) gear (if your bike has two chainrings), or high, medium, and low gear (if it has three chainrings). Use high gear for going fast or for descending on hills. The middle gear is used most frequently because it is good for flat terrain as well as for slight inclines and descents. Use low gear to climb steep inclines. As you shift the chain closer to you, toward the inside of the bike, you will drop to a lower gear, and as you shift away from the bike, you will get a higher gear. The biggest chainring requires the largest amount of force and moves the bike the greatest distance per pedal revolution, while the smallest one requires the least amount of force and moves the bike the shortest distance per pedal revolution.

Shifting the front derailleur smoothly requires a bit of finesse. If you look at the front chainrings, you can see that they are quite a bit different from each other in size compared to the range of rear cogs and that part of the chain is in tension when pedaling. Making a shift with the front derailleur is easier if you momentarily let up on your pedal force. This acts to reduce the tension on the chain, increasing the likelihood of a smooth shift.

Shifting the Rear Derailleur

The rear derailleur acts as a fine-tuning adjustment for the range that you select with the front derailleur. Use your right hand to shift the rear derailleur and adjust

HOW GEARS REALLY WORK: RATIOS

Gearing uses basic math ratios. For bicycle gears, the ratio is the number of teeth in the front versus the number of teeth on the rear that are engaged, expressed as front teeth:rear teeth. A larger ratio indicates the pedal requires more force to turn. So a ratio of 40:8 (or 5:1) is harder to turn than 30:15 (2:1). So, in general, a high gear combination of the larger ring in the front and the smaller ring in the back makes it hard to pedal. The low gear combination of the smaller ring in the front and the larger ring in the back makes it easier to pedal.

Your bike probably has fewer gear ratios than it has possible front and rear cog combinations. If your front chain wheel has three rings and your rear cassette has eight rings, you have 24 gears (3 multiplied by 8). Yet, you will notice that some gears feel similar even in different combinations of front and rear. That's because different combination will produce the same gear ratios. For instance, it is possible to have tooth combinations of 50:25 and 32:16, yet both create the same 2:1 ratios for pedaling resistance.

to smaller differences in terrain change. Shifting is less dramatic in the rear, as the chain there is not under tension, and it is generally much smoother.

Shifting the rear derailleur moves the chain along the rear cogs. The relationship of cog size to pedaling effort is the reverse of that for the front gears. To help make climbing a hill easier, you shift the chain onto a larger cog, closer to the bike frame. Shifting the chain onto a larger rear cog (lower gear) allows you to decrease the amount of force you must apply per pedal revolution and also reduces the distance the bicycle will travel per revolution. If you are riding on flat terrain or descending and would like to increase your speed, shift the chain onto a smaller cog in the cassette. This will require greater force per pedal stroke but will move the bike a greater distance per pedal revolution.

If you are in the large (outside) chainring (on the front wheel), it is not generally advisable to shift into the largest cog in the rear. This is called **cross gearing** and puts unnecessary stress and wear on the chain by stretching it sideways across the length of the drive train. Likewise, it is not good to ride in a small–small combination. Find a comparable gear using the middle ring instead.

CONTROLLING YOUR BICYCLE

Now that you have the basic riding skills, it's time to improve them. Here are some basic concepts that will help you go a long way in becoming a confident road cyclist. Mastering these concepts, including balance, scanning, riding with one hand, and signaling, will enable you to interact with other traffic confidently and securely. These are slightly more advanced skills, so be sure to practice them often in a low-traffic setting before trying them out on the road.

Balance

Bikes in motion go forward; bikes that stop fall over. While this might be simple physics, it is an important concept to know when learning to handle your bike. For example, it is actually easier to practice skills and balance when going a bit faster than when you are going very slowly. Because of the challenge presented by slow speed, it's important to practice maneuvers while moving slowly.

Balance on the bicycle is a learned skill. If started in motion carefully, a bicycle without a rider can coast all the way across a parking lot before it eventually falls down. On a bike that is moving and upright, the wheel tends to line up and stay in the direction of motion. This explains why riding a bike without touching the handlebars is simply a matter of leaning the bike in the direction you wish to travel. Many people can turn their bikes without placing their hands on the handlebars (not advised for beginner cyclists). This advanced maneuver demonstrates that balance on the bike controls the bike more than your hands holding the handlebars. Balance is easily practiced on a long blacktop stretch or a traffic-free street.

If the bike leans to the right, the front wheel will tend to steer itself to the right, and if the bike leans to the left, the wheel will steer to the left, assuming no force is applied to the handlebar. As you ride, try using small motions to steer the front wheel as little as possible, keeping the bike directly under your center of gravity. Look up and ahead and let the bicycle work for you.

Scanning

Communicating your intentions with body movement, eye contact, and hand signals is essential to predictability. Scanning back for traffic is used in many situations and helps you assess your surroundings so that you can plan for a predictable path. Scanning is the act of looking over your shoulder, and it has two primary purposes. It helps you to visually assess your surroundings, including what's behind you. And as a form of body language, scanning indicates to motorists or other cyclists that you may want to change your speed or roadway position. To successfully do both of these things, you must learn to look back for more than a mere flash. You need to be able to look back for a few seconds while maintaining your speed and keeping the bike straight and steady. Scanning is so important for cyclists that you should consider it an art form, one that is worthy of practice and attention. Practice looking over each shoulder until it becomes second nature and you are able to maintain a straight line of travel while looking back (figure 4.3).

Riding With One Hand

Riding with one hand is also an important skill to master. Cyclists need to use a free hand to signal turns, make strong hand gestures to signify intentions, and drink water. Riding with one hand is a fairly basic skill to learn and practice.

When practicing, start riding at a decent pace and place your left hand on your left hip. Leaving your right hand on the handlebars allows you to gently squeeze the rear brake if necessary. Also, you will take your left hand off the handlebars more frequently than your right for scanning and signaling purposes.

Try riding in a straight line first and then graduating to easy turns. Eventually you want to be able to pedal uphill with your left hand off the handlebars so that you can indicate a lane change and merge with traffic approaching from behind.

Figure 4.3 Scanning over your shoulder while continuing to travel in a straight path takes some practice. As with all safety maneuvers on a bicycle, it is important that you master this skill *before* you try it out in traffic.

When practicing a scan back to the left (the typical direction of a scan), use your one-handed riding technique. With your hand on your left hip, look back and keep your pace constant. You can now see how placing your hand on your hip stabilizes your body and helps you keep the bike moving straight and forward while you are looking back. Shifting your hand to your hip is a strong visual movement, and it will straighten your torso so that motorists can see a clear change in riding position. Now, when looking back, you can make clear eye contact and can wave or point your (left) free hand to show that you plan on entering into the traffic lane. If it comes down to it, you can give a straight arm and forceful open hand gesture to the motorist to negotiate a merge.

Practice this skill on a blacktopped playground with a straight line painted on it. The line will help you determine how far you are swerving. Try scanning with both hands on the bars too. It is possible that two hands will be easier for you, especially if you are not yet confident riding with one hand.

Signaling

The three basic hand and arm signals are left turn (left arm straight out to the side like you are pointing left), right turn (the left arm bent upward at the elbow, or the right hand pointed straight out to the right side), and stop (the left arm bent downward at the elbow). For more details about these signals, see chapter 3.

Hand and arm signals should be made at least 100 feet before a turn. If the road surface is rough or you would put yourself in danger by taking your hand off the handlebars, you are not required to signal when driving a bicycle.

Kid's-Eye View

Bicycle Handling Skills

Children generally learn the balance and confidence needed for their first bike ride in a series of phases from tricycles to balance bikes. Small children (under seven years) can usually benefit from a parent's encouragement.

An easy way to teach a child to ride a bike is to use a balance bike. Balance bikes are lightweight and have no pedals. You can make a balance bike by removing the pedals from a child's bike, lowering the seat, and encouraging the child to push the bike like a scooter while on the seat, coasting with both feet near the ground. The child can easily stop herself and hold herself upright when she starts to feel unsure. Be careful, though: If the bike has coaster brakes, whereby you stop by pushing backward on the pedals, removing the pedals takes away her braking ability. If you use a large, open area, watch carefully to ensure your child is not gaining too much speed. The length of time she can coast should grow until you are ready to put the pedals back on. By then, the balancing will have become natural, and your child will have the hang of it.

Children should learn to stop before entering the roadway. It is very important that they look left, then right, and then left again before proceeding. Children tend to ride on sidewalks, so driveways, sidewalks, and crosswalks are potential danger zones.

To teach children to ride in a straight line, use a painted line in a parking lot. Straight-line riding allow drivers to predict what the child will do. Predictability is important in any traffic situation; kids don't know this.

In addition to hand signaling, freely use body gestures to let other road users or pedestrians know your intentions. For example, if a car has the right-of-way, try waving the driver on, to indicate your intention to yield. This level of communication increases your predictability and may help calm uncertain car drivers. Consider waving a signal of "thanks" or "no, thanks," to your fellow road users.

Bicyclists use all of their senses while bicycling, and they may as well use their voices as well. Speaking to inattentive pedestrians is an effective way to get their attention or assure tentative walkers that you plan to yield so they can cross. Telling a pedestrian to cross at any given corner is not only courteous but may prompt them to move quickly, preventing you from having to come to a complete stop.

CONCLUSION

From getting on your bike to signaling your intentions to drivers, this chapter has covered much of what you need to know to ride a bike successfully. While it may sound intimidating to talk about what actually happens during a turn, or how to signal and scan, in practice many cyclists find these behaviors to be second nature.

AVOIDANCE
MANEUVERS

nfortunately, riding your bike defensively, driving your bike carefully, and following all the rules of the road don't ensure that you will never be in a tight situation. You can't control other drivers, road conditions, or the weather, and these factors can rear up and become dangerous in a moment. The maneuvers in this chapter are important to practice, vital to know, and—it is hoped—rarely used.

CAUSES OF CRASHES

About 50 percent of bicycle crashes are falls that do not involve another vehicle (Kaplan 1975; Moritz 1998). Dogs, children, gusts of wind, railroad tracks, steel grates, steel patch plates in the pavement, ice, and slick pavement are all potential

---

ABC QUICK CHECK

A Is for Air

Inflate tires to rated pressure as listed on the sidewall of the tire. Use a pressure gauge to ensure proper pressure. Check for damage to tire tread and sidewall; replace if damaged.

B Is for Brakes

Inspect pads for wear; replace if there is less than an eighth-inch of pad left. Check the pads for adjustment; make sure they do not rub tire or dive into spokes. Check brake lever travel; there should be at least one inch between bar and lever when applied.

C Is for Cranks, Chain, and Cassette

Make sure that your crank bolts are tight; lube the threads only and nothing else. Check your chain for wear; 12 links should measure no more than 12 1/8 inches. If your chain skips on your cassette, you might need an adjustment or a replacement.

Quick Is for Quick Releases

Wheel hubs need to be tight in the frame; your **quick release** (a cam mechanism that allows the wheels to be removed quickly and without any tools) should engage at a 90-degree angle. Your front hub quick release should point back toward the rider to ensure that nothing catches on it, and the rear hub should close into the angle of the frame. Inspect brake quick releases to insure that they have been re-engaged.

Check Is for Check Over

Take a quick ride to check if the derailleurs and brakes are working properly. Inspect the bike for loose or broken parts; tighten, fix, or replace them. Pay extra attention to your bike during the first few miles of the ride.

hazards to cyclists. Falls are caused by mechanical failure too, so the first thing to do before you ride is perform an ABC quick check on your bike (see the sidebar on p. 58). Once you have checked out your bike for safe travel, stay alert to hazards on your ride and use extra caution when you sense they are present.

The three basic classifications of hazards are surface, collision, and visual. Surface hazards include glass, storm grates, potholes, railroad tracks, and slick pavement from rain, ice, oil, or leaves. Collision hazards include turning cars, other bikers, walkers, dogs, curbs, and trains. (Remember to watch out for parked cars, too.) Visual hazards are things that may block a bicyclist's view, such as bushes, fences, trees, sharp turns, or cars.

The most serious type of fall is the one caused by a sudden stop that vaults you headfirst over the handlebars. When pedestrians and animals appear suddenly in your line of travel, you must decide quickly how to deal with the situation. Always maintain control of your bike so that you can react quickly. When riding in urban settings, keep both hands on the handlebars in the braking position for best control.

When you find yourself riding over or near hazards, you can apply the **front-wheel principle**: the stability of the front wheel dictates the stability of your bike. Generally, if you are riding toward a hazard that is totally unavoidable, try to at least avoid it with your front wheel. If avoidance isn't possible and your front wheel sticks in a hole or railroad track, your best bet is to hold the handlebars firmly and pedal out. Once your front wheel is totally stuck or out of control, you are likely to fall.

Surface Hazards

Stay alert to the road surface and hazards that may be present (figure 5.1). Extra care needs to be taken when riding over metal obstacles, as they can be very slippery. Proceed slowly and do not brake or turn quickly on metal grates, plates, or slats. Water over the road can cause dangerous conditions. The narrow and slick tires of road bikes are more susceptible to failure on these types of hazards; wider tires on your bike are one way to improve stability.

Railroad Tracks

Be conscious of the angle of railroad tracks as you approach them. When approaching railroad tracks, scan for traffic and move into position to cross with your wheels at a right angle to the rails. It is also a good idea to stand up and let your legs and arms act as shock absorbers. Railroad tracks, cracks in the pavement, and grates are common causes of diversion falls, which occur when your front wheel is diverted or trapped and you are unable to steer your bicycle back under you.

Steel Plates

Steel plates are used by construction crews to cover work in progress. They can have sharp edges running parallel to your travel that will steer your bike out from under you, or they may have sharp edges facing you that you have to roll over. If this obstacle cannot be safely avoided, sit back and take the weight off your front wheel while being careful to keep it straight. These obstacles can also cause a **snakebite flat**. (This is the result of tube damage characterized by two small slits. It is usually caused by hitting a sharp edge such as a construction plate or pothole on underinflated tubes and pinching the tube against the rim.)

Figure 5.1 Surface hazards can pop up anywhere, from a new pothole on a familiar street to recently installed rumble strips.

Storm Grates

Storm grates and sewer drains are slippery when wet. Some designs may have slots that can trap your front wheel. Exercise caution when riding over grates. If at all possible, avoid them.

Surface Cracks

A long, narrow pavement crack running parallel to your path of travel can steer your bike out from under you if it catches hold of your front tire. In order to avoid this type of hole or crack, change your path of travel to cross the crack at a right angle. Be sure not to move suddenly into the path of another vehicle—scan behind you before moving left into traffic if you need to do so in order to avoid a surface crack.

Uneven Road Surfaces

Uneven road surfaces need to be addressed just like a railroad track or pavement crack. Turn your wheel to cross onto a different level of pavement at a right angle.

Wind Blasts

While wind isn't technically on the surface, it is considered a surface hazard. Gusting wind and gusts caused by vehicles can come up suddenly and affect cyclists. The front of large trucks can blast you away and then suck you in as they pass you. You need to correct the lean caused by a wind blast, so maintain sufficient space between yourself and other vehicles, claiming the lane if necessary. Hold the handlebars firmly and lean slightly to compensate for the effect of any gust. Practice and experience will help you gain confidence in dealing with wind blasts.

Collision Hazards

One of the many reasons for avoiding riding on sidewalks is the drastically increased risk of collision hazards. Because vehicle drivers are not expecting cyclists on sidewalks, they are more likely to turn in your path (figure 5.2). You also have an increased risk of hitting a pedestrian or an unexpected crack in the pavement. The following are some common collision hazards.

Figure 5.2 From dogs to taxi cabs pulling in front of you in the bike lanes, collision hazards are a constant concern for cyclists.

Dogs

When a dog is chasing you, the most serious risk is a collision with the animal. Speak in a loud voice and continue to move away from the dog's territory. Keep riding and talk to the dog to let him know you are human, or dismount and put the bicycle between you and the dog. You should always report dog attacks or chases.

Turning Cars

Drivers of motor vehicles may not be looking for bicyclists. When you see a car is going to turn into your path, be sure to signal to indicate you are there. If you cannot make eye contact, slow down: You may have the right of way, but it is better to be safe than sorry.

Other Cyclists and Pedestrians

Pedestrians have the right of way in most situations, whether interacting with a car or a bicycle. They also tend to walk the shortest distance between two points, which means cyclists have to deal with pedestrians darting out from unexpected places. The best way to interact with other cyclists and pedestrians is to look ahead and be prepared.

Visual Hazards

Even if you know the route you bike very well, visual hazards are a problem. From parked cars that obstruct your view to growing bushes, fences, or trees, these hazards are a constant problem (figure 5.3). You may need to slow down or adjust your position on the road to remain visible.

Fences, Bushes, and Trees

These three visual hazards are a question of sight lines—they can block your vision on driveways, parking lots, and side streets. In these conditions, you must slow down and prepare for other vehicles that may be coming across your path.

Sharp Turns

At a sharp turn, especially to the right, you may not be able to see other oncoming vehicles. Move more to the left at sharp right turns so you can see around the curve earlier.

Other Vehicles

Other vehicles can block your view of approaching hazards, such as potholes or an oil slick. They also may block your vision of oncoming traffic. Always slow down when traveling close to other vehicles.

Figure 5.3 Overgrowth on trails can block important information, oncoming traffic, or worse.

Motor Vehicles

According to a study sponsored by the National Highway Traffic Safety Administration (Cross and Fisher 1977), a cyclist's actions that most likely result in a crash with a motor vehicle include the following:

- The bicyclist enters a roadway from a driveway, alley, or over a curb or shoulder without slowing or stopping for traffic on the roadway (failure to yield right of way).
- The bicyclist rides into an intersection against the stop sign, yield sign, or traffic signal (failure to obey traffic control device).
- The bicyclist rides against traffic (failure to keep right).
- The bicyclist rides at night without lights (inadequate equipment).
- The bicyclist makes a left-hand turn or swerves into the traffic lane without signaling or looking for approaching traffic (failure to signal or yield right of way).

For adult cyclists, the cause of collisions is about evenly divided between motorist and cyclist error (see table 5.1). When collisions involve child cyclists, the error is more often made by the cyclist. Motorists tend to err in the following ways:

- Turn right or left into the path of a cyclist (failure to yield right of way).
- Enter the roadway from a driveway or intersection (failure to yield).

Table 5.1 Causes of Motorist–Cyclist Collisions

Who is at fault?	Action	
Bicyclist	Riding facing traffic (not with traffic)	14%
Bicyclist	Left turn from the right side of the road	11%
Bicyclist	Failure to yield from driveway	9%
Bicyclist	Running a stop sign or signal	8%
Bicyclist	Swerving in front of car	5%
Total bicyclist		**47%**
Motorist	Left turn in front of the bicyclist	13%
Motorist	Right turn in front of the bicyclist	11%
Motorist	Running a stop sign or signal	8%
Motorist	Opening car door into path of the bicyclist	7%
Motorist	Failure to yield from driveway	6%
Motorist	Didn't see the cyclist	3%
Total motorist		**48%**
Undetermined		**5%**

The highlighted lines are the only crashes that involve cyclists hit from behind.

From Kaplan 1975 and Moritz 1998.

- Overtake a cyclist—either too close to or unaware of the presence of the cyclist (failure to yield).
- Misjudge the speed of cyclists, mistakenly believing they have adequate time and distance to turn left in front of oncoming cyclists.

Motorists may be more conditioned to look for larger vehicles and are less cognizant of bikes. Even when cyclists ride competently, they must be on the alert for incompetent motorists. As with all vehicles, drive defensively.

Riding on Wet Surfaces

Riding in the rain or when surfaces are wet requires extra caution. Even well-maintained brakes require increased stopping distance. You should apply your brakes well before you need to stop to scrub debris and water off the rims.

Manhole covers, drainage grates, railroad tracks, construction plates, and other metal objects get very slippery when wet. You can still ride on wet metal surfaces, but do not attempt to stop or turn sharply when either of your wheels is on them. Lane markings also can also be slippery. Crosswalks, yellow and white lines, and turn-lane markings can all become very slippery with the addition of some rain or snow. Avoid riding through puddles, as you never know what they may conceal.

PREVENTING CRASHES

Approximately 50 percent of all bicycle crashes are falls (Kaplan 1975; Moritz 1998). They are often caused by road surface hazards—impact with potholes or storm grates, or skidding on wet manhole covers, loose gravel, or dirt—or by the front wheel being diverted by railroad tracks, expansion joints, or other cracks in the pavement. To avoid these, be alert to the hazards. Be careful while turning, braking, or accelerating on a slippery surface. Steer around hazards if you can; the rock dodge technique discussed later in this chapter allows you to do this quickly, as necessary.

Research into bicycle crashes has shown that bicyclist crash rates decrease with experience measured by miles or years of cycling. Bicyclists who ride regularly under adverse conditions (rain, darkness, in the mountains, and the like) tend to be more experienced and have lower crash rates than fair-weather riders.

There are preventive measures that you can take to reduce the likelihood of a crash and avoidance techniques to learn and use if a crash is imminent: Be visible, be alert, be predictable, and be assertive.

Be Visible

Always wear bright clothing to increase your visibility during the day, and use retroreflective clothing or gear and proper lights (white in front and red, preferably blinking, in the rear) at dawn, dusk, or night. Ride predictably where you can be seen. Never ride against traffic. Avoid riding in motorists' blind spots.

Be Alert

Use constant scanning to regularly assess your surroundings. Try to make eye contact with drivers at intersections to make sure they are aware of your presence. Be aware of overtaking motorists in high-traffic situations.

Learn to recognize the often subtle signs of motorists' intentions and try to anticipate their actions. Here are examples:

- A driver may not use turn signals when stopped at an intersection, but you may notice the front tires shift in anticipation of making a turn.
- When riding down an urban street, listen for the sound of car doors being opened in front of you by motorists who have not looked behind them.
- If you see a parked car or another obstacle ahead of you, be prepared for cars to swerve to avoid it.

Be alert to oncoming motorists making a left turn across your path. Motorists often misjudge the speed of oncoming cyclists and turn into them. Make eye contact when approaching a motorist positioned for a left turn ahead of you. Continue pedaling, because you have the right of way, but prepare to take evasive action if the motorist fails to yield.

Avoid motorists making a right turn in front of you. Right-turning motorists may turn to the right just after overtaking a cyclist or another road user.

Avoid motorists pulling into your line of travel from a side street. Make eye contact with motorists if you can, and be prepared to evade them if they fail to yield.

In all cases, be prepared to take evasive action, such as an instant turn or a quick stop.

Be Predictable

Maintain a straight line unless you need to execute an instant turn or a quick stop. Keep pedaling. The motion of your pedaling is an indication to motorists that you intend to continue going straight. Do not pass motorists or other cyclists on the right. Do not position yourself in a lane that does not go to your destination. If the right lane becomes a designated right turn lane, scan over your left shoulder and move to the right side of the through lane if you're going straight.

Watch the front wheels of motor vehicles and look for other signs that indicate turns. Ride far enough away from the curb to discourage unsafe passing and to give yourself escape room if you need it (about 3 feet). Riding this distance from the right side of the roadway allows you to be easily seen by motorists entering roadways.

Be Assertive

Use hand signals, a bell, your voice, lights, anything to get the attention of motorists. Be prepared to yell loudly to announce your presence and get a motorist's attention before he moves. An attitude of confidence goes a long way. Without being rude or impeding traffic, you can occupy space in the roadway, and motorists and other cyclists will respect your right to that space. You can yield for overtaking motorists where it is safe for you to do so. Plan to take your right of way, but be prepared to act to avoid a collision. Always be aware of a safe route out whether you expect to use it or not.

AVOIDING HAZARDS

Riding safely on the road requires knowledge and understanding of traffic laws and the principles that determine and govern these laws. However, even when you ride predictably and occupy your proper place on the roadway, situations may arise that necessitate maneuvering to avoid hazards or collisions. The ability to execute an evasive maneuver could mean the difference between a close call and a crash. Be sure to practice these often. For any of these maneuvers to work when you need them, it must come naturally. Practice these moves in a no-traffic area.

Quick Stop

When you are riding in traffic and something stops suddenly in front of you, you need to bring your bicycle to a quick stop, keeping your bike under control and stopping in a short distance. There is an art to stopping a bicycle in an emergency.

When you apply the front or rear brake, the bicycle begins to slow down, and your weight transfers forward. The more weight on a wheel, the more effective the braking and the less likely it is to skid. Most of the time you can stop your bike comfortably without skidding or sliding. If you need to stop in an emergency, you may need to make a quick stop to avoid hitting an object or entering a dangerous situation. However, if you brake too quickly, the hard braking can pitch you over the handlebars.

When braking hard, slide toward the back of the bike to counteract the weight shift. Braking with the front brake about three times harder than the rear and shifting your weight back over the rear wheel will help you achieve a safe, rapid deceleration (figure 5.4). If the rear wheel starts to skid, ease up slightly on the front brake. Such a rapid deceleration is not the safest way to stop under normal conditions. In normal situations, it is better to apply brakes well in advance and signal your intention to come slowly to a stop without skidding. Skidding wears your tires, increases stopping distance, and deprives you of control of the bike.

Figure 5.4 The important part about a quick stop is throwing your weight over the back tire.

Kid's-Eye View

Avoidance Maneuvers

The Chaos Box is designed to teach children why we have traffic laws and the importance of obeying the rules. This should be taught only after riders have had a chance to practice bike-handling skills. For a Chaos Box, put one rider at a time in a section of a parking lot with instructions to ride anywhere they want, not touch a foot to the ground, and just have fun. Keep adding riders until one of two things happen: If gridlock occurs, have all the riders stop where they are and ask them what happened. Ask what would happen on the road if all the car drivers could go anywhere they wanted. Then have them all start going in a circle, staying to the right. If they all start flowing in the same direction, have all the riders stop where they are and ask them what happened. Ask them if this is the way that traffic works on the road.

Here are tips for an effective quick stop:

- For a fast, safe stop, use both brakes. This produces the optimal deceleration. If the rear wheel starts to skid, ease up slightly on the front brake. With practice, you will use the front brake harder (up to three times harder) and the rear brake more lightly to decrease your stopping distance.
- Braking with the rear brake alone will help prevent pitch-over, but it is not very effective.
- In theory, you can stop fastest with the front brake, but an error will pitch you over.
- When braking hard, slide your body back on the saddle as far as possible. You can transfer even more weight to the rear wheel by moving your rear end straight back and placing your stomach on the seat.
- When carrying a heavy load on the rear of your bike, you will be able to brake harder with less danger.

Rock Dodge

A **rock dodge** is a maneuver for avoiding any small object in the road. It is an essential skill for any cyclist to master (figure 5.5). To execute a rock dodge, keep riding straight until you are very close to the object. Just before you reach the object, turn the handlebars suddenly to the left—without leaning—so the front wheel goes around the object. Immediately straighten out and keep riding.

When you steer to the left of the rock, you automatically lean right. When you straighten up, you bring the bike back under you. Your front wheel snakes around the rock, your back wheel passes on the other side, but your body and handlebars have barely moved. The motion is subtle and the entire action happens in a split second.

You can also perform a rock dodge by turning the handlebars suddenly to the right. Turning to the left is more instinctive and probably safer, but the maneuver

Figure 5.5 For avoiding recently spilled gravel or unexpected rocks in the road, the rock dodge is a useful skill to master.

works either way. The quick turn is the trick, not the direction in which you turn.

The rock dodge maneuver will feel unnatural at first, but with practice, you will be able to use it in an emergency. Practice by placing a sponge or half of a tennis ball in an open area, such as a parking lot or paved surface without traffic. Ride straight toward the object until you are very close, and just before your front wheel hits it, turn the handlebars quickly so the front wheel goes around it, then quickly move the handlebars straight again. Do not worry if your back wheel hits it. Remember, the key to maintaining control of your bike is to keep the front wheel stable. You need to be able to move around obstacles quickly to avoid a fall.

Avoidance Weave

The **avoidance weave** is used when you suddenly encounter a series of hazards, like potholes or rocks, that could cause a crash. The maneuver consists of a set of swooping turns. To avoid a series of hazards, look ahead past the hazards and begin a turn before you reach each hazard. Continue to look ahead and turn sharply until you are through the hazards. It's important to lean your bicycle and get into a rhythm. Don't look down at what you are trying to avoid; if you do, it greatly increases your likelihood of hitting it. While this sounds simple, it is important to practice steering through repeated turns to ensure you can do it smoothly. Turning correctly is different than simply making several turns around a series of new potholes.

Instant Turn

The instant turn is used to avoid an unexpected vehicle passing directly in front of you. In these instances, you won't have the time or space to do a quick stop. An instant turn allows you to avoid the crash and go in the direction of the vehicle. Even if you do collide, it will be at an angle, and the consequences will be less severe than a head-on collision.

Many people think that a turn is produced simply by turning the front wheel, but you actually lean first and turn second. Because they happen so fast, the two moves appear simultaneous. To quickly force the lean, you have to perform a maneuver that feels unnatural and sounds even more unlikely. Turn your front wheel left—the wrong way, toward the car. By doing this you're forcing a right lean. The moment you have a lean started, turn your front wheel sharply right and you'll find yourself in a tight right turn.

This doesn't ever feel natural, and you must train yourself to do it. The quick twitch in the wrong direction at the start of the instant turn is the most important and least intuitive part of the turn. You are deliberately unbalancing yourself by steering the whole bike out from under you.

Steering toward the hazard may feel counterintuitive and require practice to master. It is important that you work on this skill because it could save your life.

CONCLUSION

These are advanced skills that require a great deal of practice. As with most advanced techniques, repetition is the key to success. These types of skills are sometimes best learned from an instructor, rather than a book. The league has a network of more than 2,000 league cycling instructors nationwide that teach the Traffic Skills 101 class. To learn more, or to find a class, go to www.bikeleague.org.

CHAPTER 6

BICYCLE PARTS AND QUICK REPAIRS

Whether you take your bike to a shop for maintenance or maintain it yourself, it's good to know a few core bicycle repairs in case you are stuck somewhere with a flat tire or loose brakes. This chapter presents an overview of some quick repairs. We'll start with maintenance items everyone should master, like lubing your chain and inflating your tires. The next points in the chapter include fixing a flat, adjusting your brakes, and cleaning your bike. Included at the end of this chapter are four checklists that summarize the steps for these repairs (pp. 83-85).There are a few more advanced repairs covered in this chapter, although not in great detail. These repairs are often best handled by a professional. If you wish to become more serious about working on your bike, there are many books on bike maintenance and repair. In addition, classes on maintenance and repair are available through the league's Smart Cycling program and at local bike shops or clubs.

REGULARLY CHECK YOUR BIKE

Before you ride, always do an ABC quick check. This is covered in depth in chapter 5, but here is a quick refresher.

- A is for air: Be sure your tires are inflated to the pressure listed on the sidewall.
- B is for brakes: Inspect pads for wear; replace if there is less than a quarter inch of pad left.
- C is for cranks, chain, and cassette: Make sure that your crank bolts are tight; check your chain for wear; and ensure the chain doesn't skip on your cassette.
- Quick is for quick releases: Tires should be secured, and the quick release should engage at a 90-degree angle.
- Check is for check over: Take a quick ride to check if derailleurs and brakes are working properly.

Grease

Any time you secure two pieces of metal together or thread metal onto metal, you need to use grease as a lubricant. Bearings also require lubrication so they don't wear down. Grease reduces friction and allows parts to move properly. A lubed bolt, such as on the crank arm, is more securely attached, has a smaller chance of coming loose, and will be easier to remove than a bolt that is not lubed.

Other bike parts that need lubrication include the **seat post** (the tubular support that holds the saddle) and seat rails; the **bottom bracket** (the part of the frame around which the pedal cranks revolve); the **headset** (the bearing assembly that connects the front fork to the frame and permits the fork to turn for steering and balancing); the brake hardware; the water bottle cage bolts; the chainring bolts; the cassette **lock rings** (thin locknuts used to keep the threaded assembly from coming unscrewed); the brake fixing bolts; and the stem (the part that connects the handlebars to the steerer of the fork) bolts. If you have a few miscellaneous creaks on your bike, it is probably due to a lack of grease. Take care not to get grease on the wheel rims or **brake pads**, however, as this will reduce your stopping power.

The chain should be cleaned and lubricated regularly with a bike-specific chain lubricant. Drip on a few drops at the cassette while turning the cranks. Wipe the chain with a dry rag while you're turning the cranks and reapply. Less is more when it comes to chain lube, as excess lubricant attracts dirt. If you are regularly going on longer rides, then you might clean and lubricate the chain every other ride or as needed to keep the chain from squeaking, wearing out prematurely, and creating drag. If you are riding frequently in wet or muddy conditions, make sure to keep the chain clean and lubricated.

Tire Air Pressure

Always follow the manufacturer's recommended tire pressure range printed on the sidewall of the tire (figure 6.1). Air pressure greatly affects the handling of a bike. Mountain bike tires are wide and knobby for increased traction in the dirt. They are designed to work best between 30 and 65 **psi** (pounds per square inch). With lower air pressure, you may get a flat as soon as you hit a root or a rock. If you exceed the recommended air pressure, you will have less control of the bike when you need it most: while climbing, on corners, at speed, and on steep descents.

Road bikes are affected by air pressure as well. Road bikes generally have tires that are rated from 90 to 130 psi. The higher the pressure, the smaller the point of contact between your tire and the road, resulting in a faster ride (less rolling resistance); but as with mountain bike tires, you should always follow the manufacturer's recommendation for tire pressure. Overinflation can reduce your control of the bike and cause tubes to explode. Inadequate pressure will result in a slower ride and may result in pinch flats. A **pinch flat** occurs when there isn't enough air

Figure 6.1 The technique for checking air pressure in your tire is slightly different depending on if you have a Presta or Schrader valve—be sure you know which one yours is! Schrader valves are like the ones on most car tires, and you can check the pressure without unscrewing anything. They are also very wide. Narrower Presta valves are often used on high-pressure bicycle tires. You must unscrew a locknut before you can check the pressure.

in the tube, and the tube gets caught between the pavement and the rim of your wheel. You'll know it is a pinch flat because there will be two holes where the rim pinched into the tube.

TOOLS FOR THE ROAD

Deciding what to bring with you on your bike ride can mean the difference between riding and walking. Knowing how to use your tools is just as important. If you don't know how to use a tool, take the time to learn. Most bike repairs are simple to do. Except the pump, which usually mounts to your frame, most tools you need will fit into a seat pack under your saddle. Some of the tools that you may want to carry with you on your rides include the following (see also figure 6.2):

- Pump: A pump is a must because there is always the possibility that you will get a flat. The use of carbon dioxide (CO_2) cartridges has also become popular in place of pumps. If you use CO_2 instead of a pump, bring at least one spare cartridge. If a quick change is the most important aspect of your planning, carry a pump just in case. Pumps can mount to the bicycle frame or can be carried in a pack, on a bike rack, or even in a jersey pocket.
- Patch kit and **tire levers**: Always carry a patch kit and tire levers. If you plan for one flat, you will probably get two. You should feel comfortable patching a tube before going out for a ride so that you can avoid having to learn this skill in the dark or in the rain.

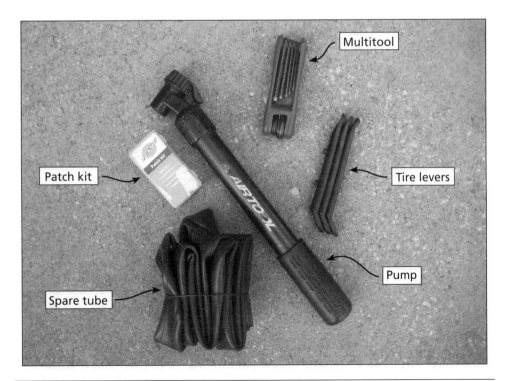

Figure 6.2 At a minimum, these are the tools you need with you on every ride. The first time you travel without them will almost certainly be the first time you need them.

- Spare tube: To save time, it is a good idea to always carry a spare tube. In the event of a flat, it is quicker to replace the punctured tube with a spare and patch the damaged tube at home later, when you will have the time to be sure that the patch is perfect.
- Multitool (including chain tool): Folding multitools include a wide range of critical tools, such as Allen wrenches, screwdrivers, and chain tools. Multitools are good to have in case of emergencies, such as a chain break. Other bike tools that are part of some multitools include a **spoke wrench**, an 8 mm wrench, screwdrivers, and tire levers. Other multitools have additional useful tools, such as knives, corkscrews, and bottle openers.
- A dollar bill or energy bar wrapper: These can be used to cover holes in tires and seal holes in shoes or seats.

ROUTINE MAINTENANCE

To keep your bike working flawlessly, it is important to keep up with routine maintenance tasks. These items range from simply cleaning your chain and rims to more complicated and time-consuming tasks such as repacking your hubs and headset. The following is a schedule of maintenance intervals to help you keep your bike in top working order. The weekly tasks are easily done by you.

Weekly

- Check tire pressure.
- Wipe down and lube chain.

Monthly

- Check rim brake pads for wear (should be showing at least one-eighth inch for the entire pad). The more brake pad on your rim, the more quickly you stop.
- Clean rims of your tires.
- Inspect tires for wear.
- Inspect frame for cracks.
- Check to make sure your wheels are **true** (that the wheels are not wobbling). This is done by standing above your bike, holding a wheel in the air, and spinning it. Look straight down at the tire as it spins and ensure it is spinning without wobbling. If it is wobbling, take it to a mechanic to have it trued—this is a tricky procedure.
- Inspect hubs, checking for looseness. Do this by moving the wheel side to side and making sure there is no play in the wheel.
- Ensure bolts and clamps are tight:
  - Crank bolts
  - Stem bolts
  - Seat post clamp
  - Derailleur fixing bolts
  - Shifter and brake lever fixing bolts
  - Water bottle cage bolts

Every 6 Months
- Replace brake pads, if worn.
- Check disc brake pads for wear.

Yearly
- Have a mechanic check cables and housing and replace if worn or frayed:
  - Brake cables and housing
  - Derailleur cables and housing

Every 18 Months
- Have a mechanic check your chain and cassette; replace if worn.
- Have a mechanic check your bottom bracket, headset, and internal geared hubs for wear.

IMPORTANT ON-ROAD MECHANICS

The bad news is that once you've been riding for any length of time, you'll surely experience a breakdown on the road. The good news is that most bike breakdowns can be quickly and easily handled without a mechanic and with just the tools you carry on your bike. In this section we'll discuss how to repair a flat and adjust your brakes.

Fixing a Flat

Flat tires happen to everyone sooner or later. There are three types of flats: puncture flats, pinch flats, and other types of flats.

- A puncture flat is caused by something sharp, like a tack, a glass shard, or a thorn penetrating the tire and the tube.
- A pinch flat or snakebite is caused by riding over an edge like a steel plate or a pothole. The tire is flattened against the rim and the tube is torn by the impact. The tube will show two parallel slits. Tires that are not inflated to the recommended pressure are especially prone to this kind of flat.
- Other flats are caused by improper remounting of the tire, worn out or damaged tires, or rim tape failure that exposes sharp surfaces that can puncture the tube. Rim tape is what covers the ends of the spokes so they do not puncture a tube—when the tape fails, punctures are very likely.

Fixing flat tires can be the most frequent maintenance you do on your bicycle. With practice, a flat can be fixed in less than 10 minutes (figure 6.3). You will need to carry the appropriate equipment for the task: tire levers, spare tube, pump, and patch kit. By being patient and following the procedure, you will reduce the likelihood of getting a **follow-flat** (a second flat that succeeds an improperly repaired flat).

1. If the flat is on the rear wheel, shift to the smallest cog on the cassette. If the front tire is flat, go to step 2.
2. Release the brakes to allow the tire to clear the brake pads.

Figure 6.3 To change a flat tire, *(a)* first remove the wheel, then *(b)* use tire levers to take off one side of the tire. *(c)* Next, remove the tube and replace it with a new one. *(d)* After putting in the new tube, check that it is not pinched under the tire, and *(e)* then pump up the tire. *(f)* Finally, put the wheel back on your bike, and don't forget to reconnect your brakes!

3. Rotate the wheel slowly to check for any obvious causes for the flat and mark with a crayon or pen.

4. Release the quick release or nut and unscrew until the wheel is free.

5. Remove the wheel.

6. Deflate the tube completely. If you have a **Schrader** valve, push the valve pin in. If you have a **Presta** valve, first unscrew the nut, and then push the valve pin in.

7. Push one bead of the tire toward the center of the rim around the entire wheel. On the side of the rim opposite the valve, insert tire levers and pry the bead out of the rim. Two or three spokes further around, insert the second tire lever. If necessary, insert a third tire lever.

8. Pull one of the tire levers all the way around the rim, removing one side of the tire. Do not remove both sides of the tire from the wheel rim.

9. Starting opposite the valve, pull the tube from the tire—keeping the relative positioning of the tire and tube intact.

10. Inflate the tire with enough air that you can find the hole by feeling or hearing the air escape. Follow the instructions in your patch kit to cover the hole in the tube with a patch. The location of the hole in the tube will tell you where to look in the tire for the cause of the flat. You can also carefully run your hands around the inside of the tire to find the offending object. Remove the object so that it doesn't immediately cause another flat! If it has created a hole in your tire larger than a pinhole, you may need to insert a folded dollar bill or piece of paper to cover the hole and prevent a repeat flat.

11. Inflate the replacement or repaired tube with just enough air to give it shape.

12. Insert the tube into the tire, starting at the valve stem and then feeding it into the tire with both hands moving in opposite directions.

13. Beginning at the valve, seat the tube over the center of the rim.

14. Work the bead of the tire back onto the rim. Use your hands to avoid pinching the new tube with a tire lever. If your thumbs aren't strong enough, use the palms of your hand to roll the last part of the bead over the rim.

15. As you refill the tube, check that the tire does not bulge off the rim. Pump the tire up to the recommended pressure shown on the tire sidewall.

16. Install the wheel on the bike. Adjust any brakes you released.

Adjusting Brakes

There are three major types of bicycle brakes: rim brakes, coaster brakes, and disc brakes. The most common type of brakes on bikes are **rim brakes**. These brakes apply force to the wheel rims to stop them from turning and are available in a variety of types including cantilever, linear pull, and sidepull. (These terms refer to the different mechanisms by which your brakes are pulled onto the wheel rim to slow and stop your bike.)

Children's bikes and beach cruiser bikes tend to have **coaster brakes**. These brakes use a mechanism inside the rear hub to stop the wheel from turning and require you to push backward on the pedals to stop. These types of brakes are fairly weak for an adult rider and can fade on a long downhill slope. Coaster brakes should be taken to a shop for repair or adjustment.

RESOURCES FOR LEARNING MORE ABOUT BIKE REPAIR

- Allwood, M. 2007. *The Complete Do-It-Yourself Bike Book: Everything You Need to Know to Fix, Maintain and Get the Most out of Your Bike.* London: Carlton Books.
- Bailey, D., & Gates, K. 2009. *Bike Repair & Maintenance for Dummies.* Hoboken, NJ: Wiley.
- Langley, J. 1999. *Bicycling Magazine's Complete Guide to Bicycle Maintenance and Repair for Road and Mountain Bikes.* Emmaus, PA: Rodale Press. Distributed by St. Martin's Press.
- Zinn, L., & Telander, T. 2009. *Zinn and the Art of Road Bike Maintenance.* Boulder, CO: Velo Press.

Disc brakes for bikes, a relatively new development, have their strengths and weaknesses. They stop you quickly, in any weather, but they are more technically difficult to maintain and adjust. Disc brakes apply force to metal discs, called rotors, attached to the wheels at the hubs to stop. Like rim brakes, disc brakes are activated by hand levers. Like coaster brakes, disc brakes should be taken to a shop for maintenance or repair.

Rim Brake Inspection

This procedure is only for rim brakes; take disc or coaster brakes to your mechanic unless you are confident you can correctly adjust them. Disc and coaster brakes have more parts and are more complex to adjust.

1. Check to make sure the wheel rim and brake pads are clean. If not, wipe the rim clean and lightly sand the surface of the brake pad with sandpaper.
2. Squeeze the brake and let go quickly to ensure the cables aren't sticking within the housing. Enlist the assistance of a bicycle mechanic if you find difficulties with the cables or housings.
3. Push on the **brake hood** sideways to be sure it is firmly clamped to the handlebar. Then place your thumb between the lever and the handlebar. When the brake is fully applied, the lever should not pinch your thumb.
4. Make sure the brake arms move freely when the lever is squeezed and return quickly when the lever is released. The brake pads or arms should not rub the rim or tire when the lever is released.

Rim Brake Pad Adjustment

Proper brake pad adjustment reduces squealing and improves braking performance. As a brake pad wears, its alignment relative to the rim changes. You should regularly check the alignment of brake pads where they contact the rim and adjust them if they don't align properly. The front end of each brake pad should contact the wheel rim before the rear of the pad—this is called a **toe-in**. You'll need a 5 or 10 mm Allen wrench to adjust the pads.

1. Loosen by one turn the nut or bolt that holds the brake pad to the brake arm.
2. Wrap a thick rubber band around the back end of the brake shoe and pad.
3. While applying modest hand force to the corresponding brake lever, move the brake pads into position against the rim and increase lever force. You may have to twist the brake pad and the underlying washers to achieve this position.
4. While holding the pad in position with one hand, tighten the bolt to secure the pad.
5. Remove the rubber band.
6. Check to make sure the brake works correctly and fine-tune the adjustment if necessary.

Brake Movement Adjustment

The most common type of brake adjustment involves compensating for brake pad wear by adjusting the cables. First, make brake pad adjustments. If the brake still does not grip well or the lever travels too far, a cable that is slightly too long is the most likely cause. Adjust initially by loosening the barrel adjuster counterclockwise on your brake lever or brake until the brake engages when a three-quarter-inch clearance remains between lever and handlebars.

If the correct adjustment cannot be obtained, you should enlist the assistance of a bike mechanic to adjust the length of the cable using the binding bolt on the brakes.

Chain Repairs

Occasionally, if you switch gears too quickly, your chain will slip off. This is a quick and easy problem to repair. Just push the derailleur down with your hand to loosen the chain, then slip it back onto the chainring. Pick up your back tire and spin the pedals a few times. This should get your chain back where it was when it fell off.

If your chain actually breaks, or if it is slipping between gears, these repairs can get complex quickly. It's best to take your bike to a qualified mechanic to adjust your derailleur if your chain is slipping, install a new chain, or fix your old one.

OTHER BIKE MAINTENANCE

Once you've mastered brake adjustment and tire changes, there are just a couple of other things you need to know in order to do basic bike maintenance. This section covers cleaning your bike and the ever-important identification of noises on your bike. Listening to your bike can help you solve a problem before it becomes a costly repair.

Cleaning Your Bike

Cleaning your bike is important, and it is something that every rider can do. Cleaning your bike will also familiarize you with the parts of your bike. Like any machine, keeping your gears and chain clean and oiled will allow them to operate smoothly and prevent them from getting worn down. Keeping your wheels and brake pads clean will allow you to stop smoothly and also promote longevity.

Doing any kind of work on your bike is easier with a bike stand. It is also smart to work on your bike in a place where you can easily clean greasy dirt off the floor.

1. If your bike is caked with dirt, use a stiff nylon bristle brush to remove chunks of dried mud.
2. Use a clean rag to wipe down the chain and remove dirty lubricant. Wipe down the derailleurs, cassette, and chainrings. If a lot of dirt has built up on your cassette and chainrings, use a flat head screwdriver or metal brush to scrape it off, and then wipe the area with a rag.
3. Use a frame-cleaning product to remove dirt from your frame and create a brilliant shine.
4. Apply a thin coat of lubricant to the chain. If the lubricant is visible on the outside of the chain, you have used too much.

Avoid high-pressure washers that will force grease out of the hubs and other bearing assemblies. Use a citrus-based degreaser and a chain cleaning device to get all the old grime and oil off of your chain. Then put a light coat of chain lube on the chain and wipe it off of the outside.

You should wash your bike with soapy water, but take care not to use a high-pressure washer. A pressure washer can harm bikes that have steel parts or a steel frame. Steel can easily oxidize and rust if not dried immediately and greased. Even on an aluminum or titanium bike, high-pressure washing can force water into hubs, washing away the grease that lubricates the bearings.

Identifying Noises and Other Issues During a Ride

Just like any machine, your bike can have mechanical problems. Often you will realize the problem after you have set off on your ride. After a while the problem might start to bother you or prove to be unsafe. In addition to performing the ABC Quick Check, you can identify problems by detecting noises that emanate from your bike during a ride and paying attention if your bike feels off. This section briefly describes potential problems and explanations for fixing them. For complex work, consult a mechanic.

Clicking Sound Near Your Feet

If you hear a clicking sound near your feet, there are at least three areas on your bike that it might be at fault. Stop riding, and do the following:

- Make sure your pedals have lube on the threads and are tightened properly.
- Make sure the chainring bolts and crank arms are tightened properly.
- Make sure the quick release levers are tight.

If none of these corrections alleviates the clicking, your cranks and bottom bracket may need maintenance. As with other complex repairs, this is best done by a qualified mechanic at a bike shop.

Creaks From the Seat

Creaks emanating from the seat clamp are common. Remove the seat post from the bike by loosening the binder bolt. Remove the saddle from the seat post and grease all the parts of the clamp. Reinstall the saddle and seat post. Be sure to wipe all the parts with a clean, dry rag.

Loose Headset

If you are riding, and it feels like your wheel isn't responding when you turn the handlebars (there is a bit of wobble), you may have a loose headset. To check for a loose headset, stand the bike on the ground, hold the handlebar, engage the brakes, and, with the brakes applied, rock the bike forward and backward. If you sense some play or knocking, the headset might not be holding the fork firmly.

Never ride with a loose headset—you may cause damage to the headset, frame, or both. However, riding with your headset too tight can damage the bearing surface, a relatively delicate piece of the headset. This repair can be complex and is best handled by a bicycle mechanic.

Scraping Sound When Pedaling

A front derailleur that is slightly out of adjustment can cause the chain to rub on the cage, making a scraping sound when you pedal. Make sure the front derailleur cage is aligned parallel with the chainrings, and try to adjust the cable tension with the barrel adjuster.

Rear Derailleur Mis-Shifts

Newer components feature **indexed shifting** (which means that the shift control has positive detents or click stops that provide discrete positions corresponding to different gears) and **barrel adjusters** (small mechanisms used for making minor adjustments on brake or shifter cables). Turning the barrel adjuster should be your first approach to eliminate any skipping. The chain and cassette may also be worn and need to be replaced. Adjustments to the rear derailleur limit stop screws (two screws that set the limits of how far the derailleur can move from left to right) should be performed only by an experienced mechanic. If the low gear adjustment is off, the rear derailleur or chain could get pushed into the spokes, with severe consequences for your wheel and your safety.

Brake Screeching

A screeching sound emanating from your brakes might be caused by worn brake pads running flat against the rim. To eliminate this nuisance, toe in the pads; that is, make sure the forward edge of the pad is about 1 mm or 2 mm closer to the rim than the rear edge. See the instructions for performing adjustments to the rim brake pad, described earlier in this chapter.

Humming Sound from the Down Tube

The **down tube** is the frame tube that runs diagonally up from the front of the bottom bracket to the lower end of the head tube. A humming sound coming from your down tube area can be caused by a loose water bottle cage. To solve the problem, remove the cage, and lube the threads of the bolts. Reinstall the cage, and take your bike for a spin.

TRAINED MECHANICS

As a cyclist, it's important to know how to handle many of the issues that arise when you are riding. It's also important to know when to turn to an expert. Bicycle mechanics are trained and have years of experience in resolving many types of problems quickly and efficiently. Their time is valuable, and replacement parts can be expensive. When it comes to riding a bicycle, your safety may be at stake, so it is worth the time and money to invest in expert bicycle maintenance and repair. Always consult an expert at a reputable bicycle specialty shop when you are unsure how to make a repair or need advice. Bike shops in areas with more northern climates tend to be busier in the spring and summer, so try to schedule annual overhauls, upgrades, or other complicated maintenance work during the winter months.

Also consult a mechanic to fix repairs that you attempted and "messed up." It is possible to damage frames and components beyond repair while trying to fix them. Be careful not to overtighten bolts, for example. If you strip the bolts, they will become chronically loose.

What should you do if your only ride needs to be left in the shop for repair? Shops sometimes offer rentals, but it's always good to keep a spare bike for just such an emergency. After you grow dependent on your bicycle, you won't want to be without it.

CONCLUSION

It's more fun to talk about how to buy a bike, where to ride, and how to improve than to talk about bike repair, but knowing the rudiments of bike repair is an important part of being a cyclist. The first flat you change might take you a while, and adjusting your brakes is definitely something you learn by doing, but after a few attempts at these and the other repairs discussed in this chapter, you'll be an old pro. And an excellent cyclist!

Routine Maintenance

Weekly

- ☐ Check tire pressure.
- ☐ Wipe down and lube chain.

Monthly

- ☐ Check rim brakes for wear.
- ☐ Clean tire rims and inspect tires for wear.
- ☐ Inspect frame for cracks.
- ☐ Make sure wheels are true.
- ☐ Inspect hubs.
- ☐ Ensure all bolts and clamps are tight.

Every 6 Months

- ☐ Replace worn brake pads.
- ☐ Check disc brakes for wear.

Yearly

- ☐ Have a mechanic check brake and derailleur cables and housing; replace if worn or frayed.

Every 18 Months

- ☐ Have a mechanic check the chain and cassette.
- ☐ Have a mechanic check the bottom bracket, headset, and internal geared hubs for wear.

From League of American Bicyclists, 2011, *Smart cycling: Promoting safety, fun, fitness, and the environment* (Champaign, IL: Human Kinetics).

Fixing a Flat

☐ 1. Shift to the smallest cog on the cassette if the flat is on the rear wheel. If the flat is on the front wheel, go to step 2.

☐ 2. Release the brakes so that the tire can clear the brake pads.

☐ 3. Check the wheel for obvious causes of the flat.

☐ 4. Release the quick release or nut and unscrew until the wheel is free.

☐ 5. Remove the wheel and deflate the tube.

☐ 6. Remove one side of the tire by prying one bead from the rim.

☐ 7. Starting opposite the valve, pull the damaged tube from the tire. Keep the relative position of the tire and tube intact.

☐ 8. Inflate the tire with enough air so that you can find the hole by feeling or hearing the air escape. Patch the hole, and check the inside of the tire for the object that caused the flat.

☐ 9. Inflate the replacement tube with sufficient air to give it shape.

☐ 10. Insert the tube into the tire and work the bead onto the rim.

☐ 11. Inflate the tire to the recommended pressure.

☐ 12. Install the wheel on the bike and adjust the brakes.

From League of American Bicyclists, 2011, *Smart cycling: Promoting safety, fun, fitness, and the environment* (Champaign, IL: Human Kinetics).

Rim Brake Inspection

☐ 1. Wipe the rim clean.

☐ 2. Squeeze the brake and let go quickly to ensure the cables aren't sticking.

☐ 3. Push on the brake hood sideways to be sure it is firmly clamped to the handlebar. Then place your thumb between the lever and the handlebar. When the brake is fully applied, the lever should not pinch your thumb.

☐ 4. Make sure the brake arms move freely when the lever is squeezed and return quickly when the lever is released. The brake pads or arms should not rub the rim or tire when the lever is released.

From League of American Bicyclists, 2011, *Smart cycling: Promoting safety, fun, fitness, and the environment* (Champaign, IL: Human Kinetics).

Rim Brake Pad Adjustment

☐ 1. Loosen the nut or bolt that holds the brake pad to the brake arm by one turn.

☐ 2. Wrap a thick rubber band around the back end of the brake shoe and pad.

☐ 3. While applying modest hand force to the corresponding brake lever, move the brake pads into position against the rim and increase lever force.

☐ 4. While holding the pad in position with one hand, tighten the bolt to secure the pad.

☐ 5. Remove the rubber band.

☐ 6. Check to make sure the brake works correctly and fine-tune the adjustment if necessary.

From League of American Bicyclists, 2011, *Smart cycling: Promoting safety, fun, fitness, and the environment* (Champaign, IL: Human Kinetics).

CHAPTER 7

GEAR AND EQUIPMENT

eyond a well-maintained bicycle, additional gear will make your ride safer and more enjoyable. Gear will assist you in having a safe and comfortable ride, day or night, summer or winter, in rain or dry weather. It can help you carry cargo and enhance the usefulness of your bike as a mode of transport or as a tool for training and endurance.

You should definitely have a helmet and lock. Other gear will make your commute or recreational ride complete, such as a bike rack or water bottles. This chapter explores the wide range of gear and puts gear options into perspective so that the cost of gear does not become a barrier to cycling.

BASIC GEAR FOR ANY CYCLIST

The following pieces of gear are either necessary or highly recommended for all your bike adventures:

- Helmet
- Lock
- Gloves
- Sunglasses or other protective eyewear
- Water bottle
- Bike rack
- Lights

Helmet

A helmet is the most important piece of equipment for preventing serious injury (figure 7.1). It is crucial for safety when cycling. Not only does it protect your head and brain in the event of a fall, it makes you more visible to others. You will also be seen by children as you ride—yours or other people's—and wearing a helmet sets a good example.

If you do not own a helmet, you should purchase a good one. If you own an old one, it may be time to replace it with a newer model. Select the smallest size helmet that fits comfortably on your head. There should be little or no room between the helmet and your head on the sides, front, and back. Many helmets come with adhesive-backed or Velcro pads to help customize the fit. Some have integrated strap retention systems that permit an even more customized fit. The front of the helmet should be positioned so it sits level and covers the forehead; it should not be tilted back nor so far forward that it obscures your vision. The helmet straps should be adjusted using the plastic sliders and the buckle. Position the sliders just below and slightly in front of your ears. Remove all slack between the helmet and the sliders, and tighten the sliders down.

The chinstrap should be snug when buckled. You should only have room for one or two fingers between the buckle and your chin. If the buckle is not centered below your chin, it will be necessary to take up slack from the strap on the side of the helmet that is too long. This often requires you to readjust all of your straps, sliding the extra strap length through the back of the helmet and readjusting.

Fitting a helmet is not a one-time task. Even though straps are secured in the plastic buckles, they can creep out of adjustment over time. You may also have to

Figure 7.1 It's very important that the helmet be secure when you move your head rapidly back and forth. Test it before you ride!

readjust your helmet straps if you want to wear cold weather head coverings under your helmet. You should regularly check the fit of your helmet and take the time to readjust it if necessary.

Lock

Locks are essential for any cyclist who plans to use his bike around town. Locks come in various styles and quality: heavy-duty chain locks, cable locks, and the popular U-locks (figure 7.2). U-locks provide the greatest security because cable locks can be cut pretty easily and chain locks are much more unwieldy to carry around. U-locks can even be mounted on your bike. Two locks used in combination will go even further to deter thieves. When purchasing a lock, consider the value of your bike and buy an appropriate lock.

There is a generally agreed-upon hierarchy of locking: First, your frame must be locked. It's easy to lock a wheel or a saddle and think your bike is secure, but it is not. Thread the lock through the frame and the bike rack to ensure it is locked. If you are using a second lock, or your lock is large enough, lock your front wheel. Generally, both wheels have quick release hubs, but the rear wheel is harder to remove because of the gears. Unlocking and walking away with a front wheel take only seconds. So lock the frame and the front wheel if you can. If you are using a second lock, perhaps a cable one, use this to lock your saddle to the U-lock or chain lock you are using. It is not recommended to use only a cable lock to lock your frame and front wheel—they just aren't that secure (figure 7.3).

Figure 7.2 Chain locks, U-locks, and cable locks are all popular ways to prevent bike theft.

Figure 7.3 The best way to lock your bike is with a U-lock and a cable threaded, as shown here.

Gloves

Padded cycling gloves will help reduce the impact of cycling on your hands. The padding in the gloves helps decrease fatigue in your upper body, and the back of most gloves has a soft material that can be used to wipe sweat from your forehead. You should try on a few different types of gloves to find an adequate fit. In addition, gloves help protect your hands in the event of a fall. In general, biking gloves are fingerless to allow better movement and more air circulation. However, you can get winter cycling gloves that have full fingers.

Sunglasses

Glasses are useful for eye safety and improve your ability to see and respond to hazards and changing traffic or surface conditions. Glasses can protect your eyes from debris, insects, branches, and the sun. Wraparound-style sunglasses provide the best protection and are usually the most comfortable. Many models come with different colored lenses for varying light conditions. A number of optical companies offer sport-specific sunglasses for prescription eyeglass wearers.

Hydration on the Road

Replacing fluids lost when riding is easier if you mount a water bottle cage or two to your bike frame and slide the bottle in before your ride. The water bottle and cage is an economical option, and you do not have to carry anything on your back (figure 7.4). However, wearing a **hydration pack**, a water pack that you wear on your back with a straw that mounts over your shoulders for easy access, allows you to carry much more water for longer trips and frees up your hands. Hydration packs also have space to carry tools, food, and other supplies.

Figure 7.4 Staying hydrated is key to a successful bike ride.

Bike Rack

Mounting a rack on the rear of your bike makes your bike more utilitarian. The rack can be used to mount lights, carry a lock and bags, and strap on all sorts of items (figure 7.5). In addition, a rack can protect the rider from water the same way that a fender does, blocking the spray onto your back from the rear wheel. Add pannier bags, and you are ready to commute.

Figure 7.5 A rack comes in handy whether you are commuting, touring, or just riding around town.

Lights

In most states, it is illegal to ride at night without a white front light and red rear reflector; however, regardless of the law, you should always have these lights on your bike at a minimum. Having them will increase your safety on the road at night, enabling you to both see and be seen. Safety at night for many people goes far beyond low-powered lights and a reflector, with options from high-beam halogens to helmet lights and blinking rear lights.

Front Lights

The purpose of a handlebar-mounted light is twofold: to make you visible to others and to illuminate the surface in front of you (figure 7.6a). An inexpensive low-wattage light will make you more visible to others, but it will do little to help you see where you are going. Inexpensive lights are rather dim and require frequent battery replacement. If you are riding where there are no streetlights, or if you want to ride on dirt trails at night, you will need to upgrade your lighting system significantly.

Some commuters ride with a 3-watt, C-cell powered light. Others recommend at least a 10-watt light. You can purchase bike-specific lights that offer up to 45 watts in a single rechargeable unit, which you can install yourself. Some hubs generate power for a light, and some lights run on generators powered from the tire or wheel rim so that your own pedaling power fuels the light. If you commute regularly at twilight or in the dark, it is worth investing in a quality lighting system to make sure you can see and be seen. Rechargeable batteries are more desirable than disposable batteries due to their convenience and environmentally friendly characteristics. You can avoid regular trips to buy batteries by plugging into the wall and charging up in advance. Some of these light systems can hold a charge for more than two hours.

Rear Lights

Red rear lights (as distinguished from reflectors), while not mandated by law in all states, are one of the most recognizable bicycle features on the roadway (figure 7.6*b*). Blinkies, as they are often called, refer to a flashing mode available on most lights. Be sure to mount the lights on something stable, not on flimsy bags or packs, and where bags, panniers, fenders, or other gear on your bike cannot obscure them. Most rear lights are designed to emit light in one direction, making them almost invisible if they are not aimed directly at other road users. If you often ride at night, you should consider additional reflective devices—usually placed on your wheel spokes—that provide more visibility from the side. Be sure to wipe down the lights or reflectors after a wet or muddy ride to ensure maximum light transmission.

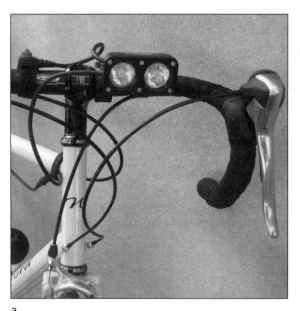 

a   b

Figure 7.6   The brighter the light, the better the visibility: *(a)* front lights; *(b)* rear lights.

Accessorize and Be Visible

Sometimes, even a blinking red light can be lost in background light. Many cyclists accessorize their bicycles and clothing or helmets with retroreflective tape, or they wear retroreflective clothing, safety vests, and hazard triangles so motorists can spot them from a greater distance. Retroreflective tape on the frame and the spoke side of the rims will make you stand out better at night. Velcro straps that go around pantlegs to keep them from getting caught in the chain are often reflective. These also have the advantage of defining motion for the driver, distinguishing you from a mailbox or other object. When riding on low-traffic rural roads, it is important to do as much as possible to make yourself visible and recognizable as a bicyclist.

BIKE CLOTHING

Bike clothing is not necessary for everyday cycling. You can ride your bike in gym shorts and a tank top, in slacks and a dress shirt, or in full Lycra. But for longer or more demanding rides, bicycle-specific clothes can keep you comfortable and increase your riding efficiency. In addition, biking in inclement weather does warrant additional thought regarding your choice of clothing.

Shorts

Bike shorts are typically meant to be worn in place of traditional undergarments. Wearing fewer layers will reduce the risk of chafing. The traditional, fitted black shorts are a popular choice. Designed with a seamless pad (called a chamois) to increase your comfort by cushioning your pelvic bones and reducing chafing in sensitive areas, the close-fitting spandex material allows greater freedom of movement on the bike and an increased level of comfort and support for your muscles.

Baggy cycling shorts are now available that provide the comfort benefits (built-in chamois) of traditional bike shorts with a bit more style and added coverage for those who feel uncomfortable wearing formfitting Lycra in public.

Jerseys

In the past, cycling-specific tops were made of wool, but today most jerseys are made of a synthetic material. Though both materials help regulate temperatures to keep you comfortable, synthetics do a better job of keeping moisture away from your skin so you stay dry and cool when it's hot and warm when it's cold. Rear pockets and zip fronts are standard on today's cycling jerseys. Many types of technical tops are available for running, hiking, paddling, and other physically demanding outdoor sports. Most of these are also suitable for cycling. Cotton holds moisture, so it is a poor choice for cool days and for long or strenuous rides.

Shoes

Your foot is the transfer point of energy between you and your bike, so shoes are an important piece of gear for serious cyclists. Though you can wear any type of shoe to ride your bicycle, a cycling or stiff-soled shoe is best. Cycling shoes have a stiff sole that resists bending so that you transmit power to the pedals more efficiently. Cycling-specific shoes help you ride longer and stronger while preventing foot fatigue and soreness. Many cycling shoes are designed so you can upgrade to clipless pedals or retention systems with cleats that fasten to cycling shoes and allow you to click in to the clipless pedals. You are better off starting out with a stiff-soled shoe, not a flexible sneaker.

Toe Clips

The addition of toe clips to basic flat pedals adds another element of efficiency to your pedal stroke. **Toe clips** hold your foot on the pedal, allowing you to pull up as well as push down on the pedals. Plastic or aluminum toe clips can be added to almost any pedal and used with almost any shoe.

Clipless Pedals

You may want to consider switching to clipless pedals if your bike currently has flat pedals or toe clips and straps. **Clipless pedals** used with cycling shoes and cleats will greatly increase your pedaling efficiency on the bike by allowing your hamstring muscles to engage more fully and connecting you more completely to your bike (figure 7.7). There is a variety of pedal systems, some designed for mountain biking and some for road riding. They have varying degrees of "float" to allow for lateral movement of the foot and ease strain on the knees. Most work like ski bindings, allowing you to easily and quickly both click in and release. If you have never ridden with clipless pedals before, you should make sure the cleat is positioned over the ball of your foot. Practice starting and stopping in a low-traffic area to make sure you are comfortable snapping in and out of them before you venture onto a high-traffic area or onto a technical mountain bike trail. Remember to anticipate the need to stop and unclip before you stop the bike.

Figure 7.7 Clipless pedals help smooth out your pedaling and increase your speed.

Cold-Weather Gear

If you are riding in temperatures near freezing, your body will work to keep your skin and core temperature regulated. You can ride in relative comfort with the proper gear. Wind chill and added cooling from evaporating sweat can cause your body temperature to drop, leading to **hypothermia**, or a subnormal body temperature. Avoid this danger by layering your clothing for insulation when temperatures dip down (figure 7.8). Layers allow you to adjust to the current climate conditions by removing or adding clothing.

For the first layer of clothing, wear a moisture-wicking layer against your skin to keep your body dry (figure 7.8a). Polypropylene, acrylic fiber, and other synthetic materials are great choices for your first layer. Avoid cotton because it keeps moisture trapped next to your skin, making your body lose heat by constantly trying to warm up the wet layer of clothing. Arm and knee warmers can be easily added or removed.

The second layer of clothing should be an insulating layer that does not absorb moisture (figure 7.8b). A polyester material or fleece would be preferable to cotton for this layer. New products and technical fabrics are developed every year to help cyclists deal with inclement weather.

The third, outer layer should be a water- and windproof jacket with little or no insulation (figure 7.8c).

Head and ear coverings are especially critical for cold-weather cycling. The straps on your helmet may need to be readjusted to make room for your hat, helmet liner, balaclava, or cap. You could also wear a wide fleece headband or ear warmers. Also important in the cold are thick gloves and glove liners; these can save your fingers from mere discomfort to serious frostbite.

Rain Gear

In many respects, riding in the rain is comparable to riding in cold weather. Layering is crucial for keeping your body dry and warm. If you have wet layers of clothing next to your skin, your body is constantly trying to heat the water while the moisture conducts heat away from your body. Prolonged exposure to wet and cold conditions increases the possibility of hypothermia. Do your best to stay dry when the temperature drops. Use breathable, well-vented rain jackets or coverings. If you are covered in a nylon shell, you may end up just as wet because the fabric does not breathe and sweat becomes trapped inside the shell.

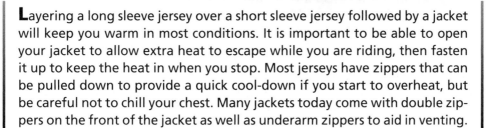

LAYERS OF CLOTHING

Layering a long sleeve jersey over a short sleeve jersey followed by a jacket will keep you warm in most conditions. It is important to be able to open your jacket to allow extra heat to escape while you are riding, then fasten it up to keep the heat in when you stop. Most jerseys have zippers that can be pulled down to provide a quick cool-down if you start to overheat, but be careful not to chill your chest. Many jackets today come with double zippers on the front of the jacket as well as underarm zippers to aid in venting.

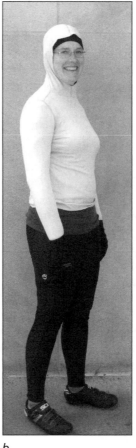

a   b   c

Figure 7.8 Starting with a warm, snug base layer and adding clothes until you have a wind- and water-resistant outer layer are key to staying warm while cycling. It's also good to be able to remove layers if you get warm while pedaling.

If there is no danger of hypothermia, riding in the rain can be a welcome change from hot, humid temperatures. Summer showers are often accompanied by cooler temperatures and decreased humidity. Make sure, however, to be cautious about the additional road surface hazards that may be caused by the rain. For example, patches of oil can become very slick when wet, and potholes are less easily detected when filled with water.

On a cold and rainy day, follow the first two layering tips described earlier in this chapter. Your third layer should consist of waterproof or water-resistant materials. Fabrics that allow your body to breathe while keeping wind and rain out are the perfect choice for the third layer. Additional gear for riding in the rain includes mudguards or fenders, helmet covers, and rain capes.

Though a bit costly, Gore-Tex is a proven foul weather fabric. Many bicycle clothing companies use waterproof and water-resistant materials in their jackets and pants, so it is worth checking with cycling businesses on the Internet or your local bike shop for the appropriate cycling apparel.

Extremities

Waterproof socks, shoe coverings, and gloves are also available to keep your feet and fingers dry. Don't try to stuff too much into a shoe, or you will risk restricting your circulation, causing discomfort. If your shoes cannot accommodate more than one pair of socks, try just one layer of wool socks and a pair of shoe covers; these come in styles ranging from thick winter neoprene booties to thin overlayers designed mainly to reduce wind drag.

ADDITIONAL EQUIPMENT

Once you're outfitted with the basics, you can add extras to your bike. While none of these is necessary for a ride, they are useful tools to use.

Bell

Some states require a bell of some type (you can find out which ones at www.bike-league.org). On a bike trail or path, it's useful to give a polite jingle before passing other users. Loud, alarming sounds such as those from air horns and sirens are counterproductive because they may startle others who will then jump in front of you. In some states, air horns and sirens are illegal.

Panniers

Perfect for hauling cargo, such as camping gear, food, or your nicely pressed work clothes, **panniers** are larger bags that attach to front or rear racks. They may affect the handling of the bicycle, so take a test ride with any new load you add.

Car Rack

The easiest way to get your bike somewhere is to ride it. If you need to transport your bike regularly, you may want to consider getting a roof rack, hitch rack, or trunk-mounted bike rack for your motor vehicle (figure 7.9). If the height of your vehicle is less than 5 feet, your best bet may be a roof rack. For a vehicle with a greater height, such as a van, stick to a rear rack. Remember to take into account the additional clearance in height or length you will need for the added bike and bike rack.

Figure 7.9   Car racks can be mounted on the top or back of the car and are usually fairly easy to install.

Trailer

Trailers can haul hundreds of pounds of cargo and will greatly increase the carrying capacity of your bicycle. Almost anything can be pulled in a trailer, but precautions should be taken to attach the trailer securely. Towing a bicycle trailer can feel like driving a truck, especially if it is overloaded with gear, so choose your cargo carefully. Give a new trailer the same kind of care you would exercise when learning to drive any unfamiliar, large new vehicle—be aware of your larger size and reduced maneuverability, and recognize the greater stopping distance you will need.

Flag

Beyond bells, lights, conspicuous clothing, and proper road positioning, a flag can boost your visibility. It is especially useful on the back of a trailer. Flags can easily be mounted on your bike in a variety of creative ways. People wear them on their helmets, mount them on bike racks, or attach them to their rear axles. As discussed earlier in the book, there is no such thing as too much visibility. Low-slung bicycles like recumbents are especially good candidates for flags, but they benefit everyone.

CONCLUSION

Don't be intimidated by the list of gear in this chapter. As we said at the outset, riding a bike is fun and easy, and it is definitely not necessary to invest in each piece of gear suggested in this chapter. However, you may find, as we have, that cycling is addictive. And the more you ride your bike, in a variety of weather, lighting, and visibility conditions, the more helpful the tools in this chapter are.

CHAPTER 8

COMMUTING BY BICYCLE

Do you have a busy schedule, but still want to keep fit? Would you like to save money and time while other students or your coworkers are stuck in traffic? Do you live within 10 miles of your school or workplace? If you answered yes to one of these questions, you are a perfect candidate for becoming a bike commuter. If your ride seems like it might be too long, try taking the bus or train or even driving a car part of the way and riding the rest. Some buses have bike racks available, and some commuter trains have cars with space especially for bikes. Even if you bike part of the way to work, you'll still save money on gas and parking.

This chapter will walk you through the commuting process, from getting your bike ready and finding a route to planning your routine once you arrive at work. Ideally, your office will embrace your new style of commuting and may even try to become a Bicycle Friendly Business. Visit www.bikeleague.org to find out more.

COMMUTER BIKES

One of the great things about commuting by bike is that, in most cases, any bike will do. Of course, you need to consider the terrain and road conditions when you choose your commuter bike. But whether you choose a road bike, recumbent, mountain bike, hybrid, cyclocross bike, tandem, three-speed, or fixed gear, the bike you are most comfortable on is probably the best bike for the job.

If you are thinking of getting a bike specifically for commuting, you may want to consider a comfort (hybrid) bike. These bikes are comfortable and easy to ride, are stable, and offer features and equipment used in commuting (figure 8.1). Such features include a wide wheelbase, thicker tires, room for fenders, and places where racks can be attached.

Figure 8.1 Riding to work is often surprisingly easy—which explains why once you get started, most commuters get addicted to riding to work.

People ride commuter bikes every day in all weather conditions. Commuter bikes are often stored and locked inside, but they are also often locked to outdoor racks and parking meters. Thus, commuter bikes take a lot of abuse as they sit in the rain and pick up grease and dirt from the city. As you might imagine, most commuter bikes are not the nicest bikes on the street. Having a dedicated commuter bike will allow you to commute without worrying about the ill effects of weather or wear and tear on a nice weekend bike. In addition, expensive, fast bikes attract the attention of thieves, while lower-end road bikes may not. (Regardless of its value, your bike should be locked securely when you leave it unattended.)

Commuter bikes generally carry more equipment than recreational bikes. You will need to plan a fairly permanent means of securing all of your items onto your commuter bike. Maintaining a separate weekend bike will allow you to enjoy the feeling of being completely unencumbered on recreational rides.

PARKING

A bike parking space is any place where you can legally and securely lock your bike. Bicyclists often use meters, newspaper boxes, trees, fences, pipes, and handrails. Ideally there should be a designated bike parking rack. The best racks have upright tubes that support your bike and provide a secure place for your lock. Finding a secure parking spot may take a bit of research, but there is usually a solution close to your destination—perhaps even in your office. If your employer does not provide secure and covered bike parking, make a formal request for a new rack.

In general, there are two types of bike parking: short-term and long-term. Short-term parking is intended for visitors and customers. A well-placed, short-term parking space is located on the sidewalk close to the door of your intended destination, in a place where people can see it, such as in front of a receptionist's window. Ideally, short-term parking should be covered, but often that is not the case. If your favorite destinations lack convenient, short-term bicycle parking racks, talk to a manager and discuss the benefits of obtaining a rack. Some city governments will subsidize the purchase price for businesses.

For commuting, you need long-term racks. Long-term racks are very secure, usually indoors or in a parking garage. Even if long-term racks are outdoors, they are always covered to protect bikes from rain and other elements. But don't let the lack of safe bike parking at your workplace stop you from commuting—ask if you can bring your bike into the workplace.

SECURITY AND SAFETY

Locking your bike in a secure location ensures that you will still have it for the ride home. Consider locking everything that might be easily stolen, such as your seat and wheels. Locks are being made in thicker, heavier U-lock styles that ward off thieves. These locks are preferable to a cable lock, which can be cut more easily. U-locks used in combination with cable locks can add to the theft deterrence of your wheels and seat post.

Locks must be used properly to secure your bike. To protect your whole bike, make sure the frame is secured to an immovable object or permanent bike parking rack. Your wheels are also expensive and, with quick-release wheels, easy to steal, so use the U-lock to lock one wheel and the frame. The front wheel is easier to remove than the back wheel, which is connected by the chain to the bike's derailleur, so be sure the front wheel is locked along with the frame.

Two other commonly stolen items are lights and seat posts. Your seat and seat post combined (it is easier to steal both at the same time) are valuable. An easy way to reduce the risk of their loss is to replace the quick-release lever with a screw nut. Some cyclists lock their seat with a cable or take it with them.

If you carry your lock on your frame, make sure it is secure. It is not advisable to carry it slung over your handlebar or locked around frame tubes. If you do this, the lock can slide when you brake and create a hazard as it impedes your steering and control. If your frame is too small to mount a lock, try carrying it on a rear bike rack or in a bike bag or backpack.

Bike commuters must also contend with limited hours of daylight. Even if there is just a slight chance that you'll be biking at or near dusk, you should look into proper lighting and reflective items to make sure you are visible. If you are riding on dark streets or unlit trails, you will also need lights to see where you are going. Lights suitable for this task will be more powerful, and more expensive, than lights that are mainly used to see and be seen. If you are not parking your bike somewhere secure (in a building or locker), you will want to take your lights with you rather than leave them on the bike.

CARRYING YOUR GEAR

Commuters carry stuff. Some carry laptops, file folders, and clothes. Others carry lunch, music, and laundry. Two questions that bike commuters must address are, "How much am I willing to carry?" and "How will I carry it?" You have a few basic carrying options: bike panniers, messenger bags, backpacks, or bike baskets.

More and more commuter and comfort bikes are available with bike baskets attached to the handlebars. These baskets are the simplest way to carry your small items, such as a purse or portfolio, and are very practical. Unfortunately, they do not offer protection from theft or the weather. Bike panniers are special bags made specifically to be transported on bike racks (figure 8.2). Experienced commuters often use panniers because they are easy on the body and avoid the damp, wrinkled clothing that a backpack produces. As the ideal solution for commuters, panniers are versatile and come in a nice variety of sizes and styles. Often sold in pairs, a bicyclist may find that only one large pannier is needed to commute each day. Though some commuters are concerned with balance, it is generally safe to ride with only one pannier. You will also have the choice between front- and rear-rack pannier setup. Because front panniers are smaller, and because your front wheel affects your steering, it is generally believed they should carry less weight than those in the rear. Waterproof panniers have also become popular, allowing commuters to ride in the rain yet avoid the worry of soaking contents at the end of the ride.

Messenger bags are popular because they are waterproof, cinch down on your back nicely, and are easy to access. Backpacks tend to be the choice for the newest commuters because that is what they already have. Backpacks are fine, but you may soon find your back wants a break, so consider the investment in a rack with panniers.

Figure 8.2 A pannier is an easy way to carry gear without loading down your back, and you can keep your lock and other equipment handy. Just don't leave it on the bike when it is unattended!

DRESS CODE

You may be interested in commuting to work by bicycle, but you are worried about arriving sweaty after all that cycling. Here are some tips and tricks to avoid becoming known as the "smelly person in cubicle 4B."

If your trip is short, you may find riding in business attire is realistic. If your trip is long, you may want to ride in more comfortable clothing and freshen up and change clothes when you arrive at work. If you choose to carry your work clothes on your daily ride, instead of folding them, roll them to help minimize wrinkling. As an alternative, you can plan ahead and store work clothing at your workplace. You can carry several days' worth of clothes in on Monday and not have to worry about wrinkles. On Friday, take laundry home in a backpack or pannier.

Take advantage of shower facilities if they are available at your workplace. If shower facilities are unavailable, give yourself enough time to cool down and change clothes before work begins. Store grooming supplies at work. You can also shower before leaving home and wipe down at work. Some folks have found that premoistened washcloths or disposable wipes are sufficient.

As another option, ask a nearby gym or health club if memberships are available for shower and locker room privileges at a reduced price. After all, you will be getting your workout on your ride to and from work. Some gyms may also offer laundry services to clean your dirty cycling attire.

ANOTHER WAY TO BIKE AT WORK

If being a regular bike commuter is not practical for you, consider keeping a bike at work for lunchtime fitness, outings, or errands. Just as some people run or go to the gym during lunch, cycling during lunch is a great way to get some exercise. Bicycling has the added benefit of allowing you to get somewhere more quickly than walking, so you can bike to a slightly distant restaurant to grab lunch, or ride over to the grocery store to pick up a few groceries for dinner.

USING A CAR AT WORK

If you are concerned about not having access to a vehicle for emergencies while at work, you may have some options to help you out. Larger companies often provide emergency rides; mass transit may be an alternative; and of course, friends and coworkers may be able to come to your assistance. There are also some *guaranteed ride home* programs in urban areas around the country that provide a taxi in a pinch. You could also drive your car to work on Monday, use the bike the rest of the week, and drive home on Friday.

Don't forget that you can use your bike for other errands, so you may not need your car for shopping after work. You may soon find yourself riding to the bank and pharmacy. Taking care of more than one stop in one trip is always valuable, so consider stopping by the market and grabbing a bag of groceries on your bike ride home.

CHILD CARE

Many parents commute to work on their bicycles with a child in tow in a bike trailer. They drop their kids at daycare or school along the way. You may be able to make arrangements with your childcare provider to leave your trailer on site so you can ride the rest of the way to work unencumbered. You may also try driving to daycare with a bike on your car, parking the car at the daycare, and riding to work from there. Another option is to alternate bicycle commuting and daycare responsibilities with your spouse.

SELECTING A ROUTE

Plan your commuting route carefully. The route you take when driving a car is not usually the same one you would want to take on your bike. Major factors to keep in mind include the directness to your destination, the number of stops, and the volume of traffic during the times of day that you will be traveling. You may want to consider using a more strenuous route for the ride home to help relieve the day's stress through pedaling. You may want to use your commute as a daily workout (a 130-pound woman burns 625 calories on a 10-mile, round trip commute), so route selection could be based on miles covered or difficulty of the roads.

Selecting your bicycle route is an important part of your riding experience. Although initially you may confine your riding to your neighborhood streets, you will eventually want to pedal across town, to work, or to the store, and you will have many road choices to make these trips. Every city and town is laid out differently, so your bicycle experience may be very different from that of a cyclist in another part of town or in another city. Regardless of where you live, finding a bike route that serves your needs is important. Once you have learned all of the traffic principles, you will have the skills required to ride on most any street. The question remains: Which street best suits your needs?

Your skills, available time, frame of mind, and personal preferences all play into your route selection. You may want to consider the following:

- Does your route include a lot of hills?
- What kind of road and traffic conditions might you expect?
- How many miles is the ride? How long will the ride take?
- Are you looking for a workout or a scenic, relaxing ride?

You may find that you have a number of route choices to your destination. Your bike map may show some designated bike routes that include streets where you normally do not drive a car and that offer quiet, slow rides. Some people prefer to move faster and choose streets with bike lanes or other through streets without special bicycle treatments. Others may choose streets not indicated on the bike map at all.

If you are a competent cyclist who operates by the basic traffic principles, you should be able to safely navigate all types of streets. At first you may prefer to minimize the amount of time that you travel on heavily trafficked streets. But your ability to confidently travel all streets will greatly extend your cycling world.

Destination-Based Routes

When you are riding for recreation, you are free to choose the nicest routes in any direction. However, every bicycle trip that you take for transportation purposes will have a destination and purpose. For these trips, you are more interested in finding the shortest distance and the quickest route.

If you have not done much destination-based cycling, start by riding to places that are easy to get to. Neighborhood destinations can often be reached by neighborhood streets. With practice, you may try to get to work or to some location that may

BIKE TO WORK DAY

Bike to Work Day, celebrated nationwide on the third Friday in May, is a great time to try commuting to work or school by bike. Because so many people commute by bicycle on this day, it's easy to find a partner to ride with or someone to show you the ropes of bicycle commuting. In addition, many communities offer free breakfasts, t-shirts, competitions, and other celebrations that make it a great day to commute. To see what is going on during Bike to Work Day in your community, visit www.bikeleague.org.

be further away or that takes you through more challenging traffic patterns. Many would-be commuters start by riding to the grocery store or a local convenience store with their backpack on.

To determine your best route, you must have a clear sense of what routes are available to access your destination. You can take the routes that you use to drive, but there are probably other routes that are more amenable than busy arterial streets.

Maps and Trail or Bikeway Guides

Looking at bikeway maps or guides can provide you with helpful information about bike routes. Bikeway maps generally provide information about streets suitable for biking, off-street paths, dangerous intersections, and perhaps elevation. You can also get directions by bike for many cities in the United States on Google Maps. Here are some good places to find bicycle-specific maps:

- City government Web sites
- Local bike shops
- Local or state bicycling organizations or clubs
- Bulletin boards at trailheads and on bike paths
- State or local convention and tourism agencies
- Libraries
- Bookstores
- Internet
- Map stores

These locations might also provide other cycling information beyond maps and guides, such as bike shop locations, some good biking tours in the area, and more.

Low-Traffic Streets

It is usually very pleasant to ride your bike on low-traffic streets. These streets are not intended as through streets for automobile use, and because of neighborhood activities, speeds are generally low. Though pleasant to ride on, neighborhood streets can also be very inefficient. Low-traffic streets tend to have frequent stops signs that require bicyclists to stop and restart their bike. In the United States, only Idaho allows cyclists to roll through stop signs, so a rolling stop is illegal and ill-advised. Neighborhoods have many collision hazards, including cars backing out of driveways, parked cars, children, and animals.

It can also be difficult to find a network of low-traffic streets. While many cities have grid street systems and are excellent for low-traffic riding, some developments feature lots of cul-de-sacs a rider would need to avoid. Most suburban developments are nice for cycling within the development, but generally all low-traffic streets lead to major arterial streets. Newer, planned communities are building extensive bicycle and pedestrian throughways while maintaining cul-de-sac streets. These designs connect neighborhood districts and are perfect for travel between you and your friend's home.

Despite the drawbacks, bicycles can travel comfortably at medium and lower speeds that are appropriate for neighborhood streets. Cruising around on your bike is a fun way to travel and perfect for accessing local businesses and other destinations.

High-Traffic Streets

Most bike networks will have a substantial set of higher traffic streets that are recommended for cycling (figure 8.3). These streets may have wider lanes, shoulders, or bicycle-specific features, such as bike lanes. But there will be other times when the only street to your destination is a high-traffic street that has no cycling treatment, and these streets require some skill to maneuver.

High-traffic streets have the advantage of being direct and speedy. Like the cars on these streets, you do not have many conflicts from smaller side streets, and you will only be required to stop at larger, signal- or sign-controlled intersections. It is generally advised to keep your cadence and speeds relatively high on major streets to fit in the traffic flow better.

High-traffic streets also require some confidence and skill to maneuver. These streets are often less pleasant in terms of noise, dirt, and pollution and can be more stressful. Also, in a crash situation, people generally sustain greater injuries when crashing at high speeds.

Figure 8.3   Cyclists follow the same rules whether riding on low- or high-traffic streets, and both places offer exciting sights and enjoyable rides.

Rural Roads

The scenery is pleasant, the air is clean, and flowers and trees abound. But this splendor comes with its challenges (figure 8.4). Rural roads, typically narrower than urban roads, often have no shoulders. Because of this narrowness, drivers often travel in the center of the road. Motor vehicle speeds are often much higher than the speeds at which cyclists are traveling. As a result, motorists have less time to react to the presence of cyclists. Horizontal and vertical sight distances are sometimes

Figure 8.4 Rural roads are very enjoyable because of their low traffic and great scenery, but they can also be dangerous when drivers of other motor vehicles are not expecting cyclists. Focus on visibility!

poor due to curves, hillcrests, embankments, and vegetation near the edge of the road. In addition, rural roads are seldom lighted at night.

Despite these concerns, there are a number of things you can do to make riding on rural roads safer and more enjoyable:

- Scan ahead for broken glass, gravel, road kill, and other surface hazards that are common on less maintained rural roads.
- Watch for longitudinal cracks or seams between the roadway and the shoulder.
- Stay visible. Wear brightly colored clothing during the day. Avoid riding at night if possible. If you must ride at night, wear retroreflective clothing and mount a white light on the front and a red light on the rear of your bike.

Streets With Bike Lanes

Bike lanes are excellent for urban riding. Bike lanes are often on high-traffic streets, providing a direct connection between different parts of towns. However, there may be laws in your area that specifically apply to bike lanes; you should research the laws in your state pertaining to such facilities. For example, some states require cyclists to ride in the bike lane if there is one available, while others allow cyclists to choose the positioning on the street that offers the best route for their destination.

Roads With Shoulders

Busier suburban and rural roads may have a shoulder rather than a bike lane in which to ride. You want to make sure you ride far enough to the right in the shoulder that motorists can pass you without having to cross the centerline but not so far to

Kid's-Eye View

Commuting by Bicycle

All of the suggestions in this chapter work whether you are commuting to school or work. There are some special considerations for young riders:

- Always try to ride with other students or parents. It is safer and you will be more visible. Some schools use "bike trains" where parents ride to school on a set route and pick up students along the way.

- Use neighborhood streets and walk your bike at busy intersections. You may want to walk along busy streets too.

- Make sure there is a good place at your school to lock your bike or store it inside.

- Obey the law, as every rider is considered the operator of a vehicle and must obey the same rules as the driver of a car: Ride in the same direction as other traffic, use hand and arm signals with stopping or turning, obey all signs and signals, make sure your brakes work, if you have to ride in the dark get lights for your bike, don't give your friend a ride unless your bike has an extra seat, and keep both hands on the handlebars except to signal.

the right that you are riding on the edge of the pavement or in the debris that can accumulate on the side of the road.

Be careful on shoulders. Their surface is often in poor condition compared to the main road surface. Shoulders can often end abruptly. Be alert so you can smoothly merge with traffic on the road.

Multiuse Paths

A lot of people feel more comfortable riding on trails or paths because they are usually set away from roadways and do not allow motor vehicles on them. Multiuse paths are also popular because they are usually surrounded by trees and enjoyable scenery. In addition, because cars are not allowed on multiuse paths, the paths are quieter than roads, allowing you to take in the sounds of nature.

While trails are often nice places to ride and many people prefer them to cycling on the road with traffic, you still need to exercise caution when riding on them. Multiuse paths are designed as a slow-paced, recreational environment. Instead of scanning for motor traffic and pedestrians, you need to scan for children, walkers, joggers, wheelchair users, in-line skaters, and other cyclists. When these paths intersect with streets, you need to take particular care crossing the street; the law rarely protects a bicyclist riding in a crosswalk, even though such grade-level crossings may frequently appear to be part of a path system. Visit www.traillink.com to find out what paved trails exist in your area.

Sidewalks

Sidewalks should be reserved for pedestrians and the youngest of bicyclists riding under adult supervision. Sidewalk bicyclists pose a risk to pedestrians as well as to themselves because sidewalks are designed for pedestrians moving at walking speed. Places where sidewalks intersect with roads and hidden driveways are especially dangerous for sidewalk cyclists, as motorists are not looking for people on bikes. Additionally, because there are no rules as to where and in which direction pedestrians should walk while using sidewalks, cyclists and pedestrians can easily collide on congested sidewalks. Check with your community's ordinance regarding bicycling on sidewalks.

CONCLUSION

Choose a nice day and give commuting by bike a try. Once you feel comfortable, experiment with riding in inclement weather. Wear rain and cool weather gear and use fenders, lights, racks, and bags to learn what works for you. Most people discover that with the proper gear, weather is not much of a hindrance. Similarly, riding to work is not as dangerous as many think. Following the bicycling principles and finding the proper equipment will lead to fun, successful commutes that promote good health and save money and time.

If you still find yourself confused or timid about cycling to work, try to find a more experienced bicyclist who can show you the ropes and find a good route. Your local or statewide bicycle advocacy group can be an excellent source of help and inspiration if you still have questions about bike commuting. Contact a local bike club, ask a salesperson at the bike shop, or search on the Internet for other local resources on bicycling.

CYCLING FOR THE FUN OF IT

Anna Kelso

In addition to being a great mode of transportation, cycling provides endless opportunities for development of physical fitness, teamwork, and interpersonal skills. Setting goals and achieving them are a great way to instill self-confidence and pride in one's own abilities. In addition, the cycling community is a very supportive environment for developing healthy friendships with people who share a common bond.

Learning more about the various types of cycling can help you determine what best suits your fitness and interests. From casual family rides to intense competition, cycling offers something for everyone. This chapter will delve into some of the more popular types of cycling, including club riding, mountain biking, touring, and competition. There are some general rules to follow for each type of riding; these may vary slightly from those for commuting or just riding around the neighborhood. Specifically, riding in a group requires more interaction with other cyclists, and there are some good tricks to learn. Mountain bicycling has its own set of rules, and then there is the wide variety of racing options. However, some people simply enjoy riding for exercise and personal fulfillment. In this case, touring or recreational rides might be more appropriate.

GROUP RIDES

Group rides are a great way to meet other cyclists in your area and get comfortable putting in more time in the saddle. Scheduled group road rides are quite common in most areas, and you can easily find a ride that suits your fitness level by contacting your local bike shop or bike club. If you are new to cycling, you will most likely want to find a ride with a relaxed pace that is around 60 to 90 minutes in length.

If you are feeling unsure of your fitness level and your ability to stay with the group, consider asking someone on the ride to keep an eye on you so that you are not dropped from the group. It is also a good idea to make sure you know the roads in your area in the event that you are unable to maintain the group's pace and need to find your way home. Should you get a flat while on a group ride, make sure to communicate this to another rider so that the groups knows to wait for you. Often, one person from the group will stop and help bring you back up to the group once you have repaired your flat. It is also good idea to get comfortable quickly fixing tire punctures before heading out on a group ride.

Drafting

Group riding is also a good way to get comfortable riding in a pack and drafting off the person in front of you. **Drafting** allows you to conserve energy by seeking shelter from wind resistance. Ideally when drafting, once you get good at it, you should be roughly 6 inches from the wheel in front of you. But if this feels too close, stay where you are comfortable. Even a distance as great as 3 feet back will give you some benefit. *Always make sure that your front wheel does not overlap with the person you are drafting.* The amount of energy saved by drafting can be as much as 30 percent, allowing you to rest before it is your turn at the front.

In a pace line (a line of cyclists drafting off each other), each cyclist takes a turn "taking a pull," or leading, while the other cyclists conserve energy in the draft. If the wind is coming from the side, the leader should rotate off in the direction from which the wind is coming in order to provide shelter for the people moving up to the front of the pace line (figure 9.1). It helps to agree on the length of time each

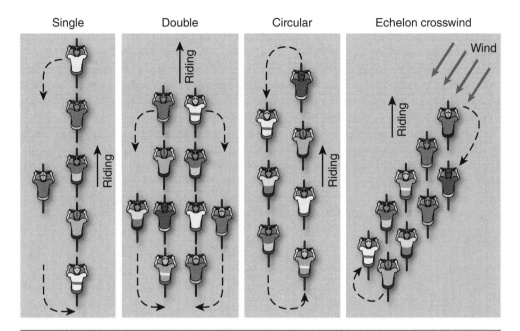

| Single | Double | Circular | Echelon crosswind |

Figure 9.1 Riding in a pace line is a great way to conserve energy while increasing speed—just don't try it until you are comfortable riding in a group and at a pace that you feel capable of sustaining.

From *Bicycling Street Smarts.* Copyright 2001 by Rodale Press. Published by arrangement with Rodale, Inc., Emmaus, PA 18098.

cyclist will pull before allowing the next person to come through. Generally speaking, pulls are usually between 30 seconds to 1 minute in length. Communicating to the rider behind you when you are ready to pull off and allow them to take the lead is often done nonverbally by flicking your elbows.

When riding in a group, it is important to communicate with the other riders about various hazards such as cars and large potholes. If you are in the front of the group, and you see an oncoming car, you will want to communicate this to the cyclists behind you by saying, "car up." Cyclists at the back of the pack are also responsible for communicating to the group when a car is approaching from behind and trying to pass. In group rides, it is common to communicate this to the other cyclists by saying, "car back." It is also important to let the riders behind you know if there is something on the road that they should be aware of, such as a pothole or glass. This can be done either verbally or nonverbally by pointing to the possible hazard. Proper communication is essential in preventing pileups when riding in a group.

Once you are comfortable riding in a pack and you feel your fitness is improving, you might want to try some of the faster, longer rides available in your area.

Organized Rides

Once you have reached a certain level of fitness and skill, you may be looking for a new challenge. You will find that the longer you ride, the more your endurance will improve. Soon you'll be riding distances that seemed daunting in the beginning. Organized rides are noncompetitive rides that provide an opportunity to ride with other cyclists who are interested in challenging themselves.

If you are interested in getting into longer distances, trying an organized **century** (100 miles) might be a good place to start. Most century ride events offer multiple distance options—50 miles, 62 miles, and the full 100 miles. Once again, building up to the 100-mile event may be sensible. Organized centuries are well supported, providing riders with aid stations along the way, as well as a **SAG (support and gear) wagon** in the event that you should have a mechanical need or become overtired. Other organized rides may include fund-raisers, mountain bike festivals, and multiday rides. Again, these are not races but rather opportunities to challenge yourself and get to know other cyclists.

Although these rides are fairly laid-back, it is still important to prepare your body for the distance. Gradually increasing the number of hours you spend on the bike from week to week can help your body prepare for the longer distances. As you increase the length of your rides, you may want to consider buying chamois cream to prevent chafing and improve the overall comfort of your ride.

TOURING

Bike touring is a great way to explore new places by bike and experience epic rides in the company of friends (figure 9.2). Some people choose to plan and organize their own bike tour while others prefer to go through a touring company. Planning your own bike tour with friends provides the added challenge of finding your route and places to stay

Figure 9.2 Some of the greatest joys of cycling come from touring—for example, cresting a challenging climb or viewing the countryside at a new speed.

along the way. Going through a bike touring company can simplify your trip and allow you to focus on the ride rather than organizing the logistics. The league also offers information on a number of touring companies both domestic and international. Each company provides different levels of support depending on the needs of the group.

Whether you are planning a bike tour for a few days or a few weeks, you will want to make sure that you have put in the proper training before you head off on your journey. In the months leading up to your trip, get in a few long rides each week in order to allow your body to adapt to the stresses you will be putting on it on your journey. You don't have to be a fast cyclist to enjoy touring; the important thing is to build up your aerobic endurance. It is also a good idea to practice riding your bike with a loaded trailer or panniers in order to get comfortable with handling a fully loaded bike. Reaching your destination after days or weeks in the saddle is a rewarding experience, and sharing this with other cyclists will provide many happy memories for years to come.

MOUNTAIN BIKING

Most mountain bikers you will meet are quite passionate about their sport, and with good cause. A mountain bike expands the possibilities of what you can do and where you can go on your bike. What once seemed intimidating and impossible soon becomes almost second nature. As your skills improve with time, you will find that mountain biking is a great way to center the mind and body. Riding the more advanced trails demands a focused mind, allowing the rider to leave behind all the stresses of the day and take each rock and root as it comes.

Not everyone is fortunate enough to live within riding distance of good mountain bike trails, but this should not discourage you from mountain biking. A good place to get information is at your local bike shop. You can also join your local mountain bike group to learn about scheduled rides in your area and carpooling options that may be available. Some mountain bike groups also offer clinics for beginners. This is a great way to learn skills that will help you on the trails and get to know other new mountain bikers in your area. Before committing to a group ride, you will want to make sure that you have selected a ride that is appropriate for your fitness and skill level.

When riding on trails, there is an accepted etiquette that should be observed. The International Mountain Bike Association (IMBA) has created a list of six basic rules that should be observed by all mountain bikers (see p. 116). Observing these rules helps to ensure the safety of other riders as well as protect the integrity of the trail system for everyone to enjoy.

Many local mountain bike groups also assume responsibility for maintenance on local trails. Service work not only helps create a more sustainable trail system but also establishes a culture of social responsibility within a mountain bike community. Participating in events such as trail maintenance days encourages camaraderie, improves trail sustainability, and provides an opportunity to get to know other mountain bikers in your area.

RACING

Bike racing not only teaches the merit of hard work and dedication but also provides a valuable lesson in sportsmanship and teamwork. With so much variation within the world of bike racing, it is easy to find a discipline that corresponds with the personality and physical strengths of each individual athlete.

IMBA Mountain Biking Etiquette: Rules of the Trail

1. Ride on Open Trails Only

Respect trail and road closures—ask a land manager for clarification if you are uncertain about the status of a trail. Do not trespass on private land. Obtain permits or other authorization as may be required. Be aware that bicycles are not permitted in areas protected as state or federal wilderness. The way you ride will influence trail management decisions and policies.

2. Leave No Trace

Be sensitive to the dirt beneath you. Wet and muddy trails are more vulnerable to damage than dry ones. When the trail is soft, consider other riding options. This also means staying on existing trails and not creating new ones. Don't cut switchbacks. Be sure to pack out at least as much as you pack in.

3. Control Your Bicycle

Inattention for even a moment could put yourself and others at risk. Obey all bicycle speed regulations and recommendations, and ride within your limits.

4. Yield to Others

Do your utmost to let your fellow trail users know you're coming—a friendly greeting or bell ring are good methods. Try to anticipate other trail users as you ride around corners. Bicyclists should yield to all other trail users, unless the trail is clearly signed for bike-only travel. Bicyclists traveling downhill should yield to ones headed uphill, unless the trail is clearly signed for one-way or downhill-only traffic. Strive to make each pass a safe and courteous one.

5. Never Scare Animals

Animals are easily startled by an unannounced approach, a sudden movement, or a loud noise. Give animals enough room and time to adjust to you. When passing horses, use special care and follow directions from the horseback riders (ask if uncertain). Running cattle and disturbing wildlife are serious offenses.

6. Plan Ahead

Know your equipment, your ability, and the area in which you are riding—and prepare accordingly. Strive to be self-sufficient: Keep your equipment in good repair and carry necessary supplies for changes in weather or other conditions. Always wear a helmet and appropriate safety gear.

From League of American Bicyclists, 2011, *Smart cycling: Promoting safety, fun, fitness, and the environment* (Champaign, IL: Human Kinetics). Reprinted, by permission, from the IMBA.

When considering which avenue of bike racing to pursue, it is important to understand the different forms of fitness and training that are required. Volume and intensity will vary depending on the type of racing you are training for. While road racing requires excellent endurance, it also demands short intense efforts, especially during criteriums (or crits). (**Criteriums** are multilap races that take place on a closed circuit with a circumference of roughly one to two miles.) Training for road races should include long road rides at slower speeds for endurance training as well as shorter rides with short sprints to increase your power. On the other hand, training for track racing should focus more on relatively short efforts at very high intensity.

Cross-country mountain bike racing is somewhat similar to road racing; it also requires a good balance of endurance and intensity, especially when trying to power up steep sections of trail. In addition, mountain bike racing requires good technical skills for maneuvering over rocks and roots or navigating down a steep descent. Gravity events such as downhill racing, dual slalom, and four-cross are short intense efforts that do not rely on endurance but demand instead short explosive efforts and extreme skill in bike handling. On the other hand, ultraendurance events such as 24-hour racing and 100-milers focus almost exclusively on endurance. Because these races are meant to be long and grueling, training primarily involves logging in long five- and six-hour rides in the months leading up to the event. A **cyclocross** race is similar to a criterium; it is a relatively short, high intensity race that also incorporates technical bike handling and a limited amount of running (figure 9.3).

Figure 9.3 Bike racing has a category, speed, and type for almost everyone.

Training

Planning for an upcoming racing season is a crucial part of proper training. The mountain bike and road racing seasons take place primarily in the spring and summer months, with races beginning in early April and continuing through late September. Cyclocross takes place during the cold damp months of fall and early winter. Generally speaking, you will want to begin training six to seven months before you intend to be in peak condition.

Early in your training regimen the primary focus should be on accumulating your base miles. This will lay the ground for the season by establishing a good endurance foundation. As the season approaches, you will gradually want to start replacing long aerobic rides with workouts designed to improve your strength and power. The duration and intensity of these workouts will largely depend on the type of racing you intend to do.

Because perceived exertion is not always the most accurate means of gauging the intensity of your workouts, many cyclists use either a heart rate monitor or **wattage meter** (a device mounted on the bicycle that measures the power of the cyclist's output) to improve the efficiency and effectiveness of their workouts. For someone who is new to racing, training with a heart rate monitor is a good place to start. Training by power instead of heart rate is a more accurate measure of excursion; however, wattage meters are significantly more expensive. Some good resources for further guidance on training are *The Cyclist's Training Bible* by Joe Friel; www.trainright.com, which is Chris Carmichael's Web site (Carmichael is Lance Armstrong's long-time coach); or www.fascatcoaching.com, which is coaching for all cyclists.

Racing Categories

For each type of racing there are well-defined categories designed to organize racers according to their performance level. Moving from one category to the next is done by accruing a certain number of points while racing.

The organization and structure of racing categories has evolved over the years and is currently sanctioned by USA Cycling. Interestingly, it was the league (under our original name, the League of American Wheelmen) that originally assumed this role in the late 1800s during the early days of bike racing in the United States. Road racing categories for men begin with category 5 (cat 5) and work up to category 1 (cat 1 and above are for professionals). Because there are fewer female racers, road racing categories for the women start at category 4 (cat 4) and work up to cat 1 and pro. Once an amateur racer gets older than 30, they will frequently race in age-defined masters categories. Prior to the 2009 racing season, mountain bike categories included beginner, sport, expert, semipro, and pro; however, this has recently been changed to coincide with the category 1 to 5 format. Unlike the road racing categories, mountain bike races also include age groups, in 5- or 10-year increments, within each category. Cyclocross races were also once categorized as A, B, or C; however, this has also been changed to the category 1 to 5 format.

Track Racing

Track racing takes place on a banked cycling track with a standard Olympic length of 250 meters; however, tracks can range in size from 150 to 500 meters. In the late

1800s and early 1900s, track racing was similar in popularity to today's NASCAR. **Velodromes** (arenas for track cycling) were abundant across the country, the most famous of which was located at Madison Square Garden in New York City. Unfortunately, this was to be the height of its popularity, as track racing was never able to rebound after the end of World War I. Today there are only 22 velodromes in the United States; however, the sport is going through a resurgence, and there are promising signs of possible velodrome construction in many urban areas.

Living near a track is quite rare, making it a difficult sport to get into if you do not have access to a velodrome. The sidebar about velodromes provides a complete list of existing velodromes throughout the country.

Within track racing there are several different racing formats that fall into one of two categories: sprint events and endurance events. Both sprint and endurance racing on the track require explosive power and keen racing tactics.

VELODROMES IN THE UNITED STATES

1. Alkek Velodrome—Houston, Texas
2. Alpenrose Velodrome—Portland, Oregon
3. Baton Rouge Velodrome—Baton Rouge, Louisiana
4. Brian Piccolo Park Velodrome—Cooper City, Florida
5. Dick Lane Velodrome—East Point, Georgia
6. Ed Rudolph Velodrome—Northbrook, Illinois
7. Encino Velodrome—Encino, California
8. Group Health Velodrome—Marymoor Park, Redmond, Washington
9. Hellyer Park Velodrome—San Jose, California
10. Kissena Park Velodrome—Queens, New York
11. Valley Preferred Cycling Center—Trexlertown, Pennsylvania
12. Major Taylor Velodrome—Indianapolis, Indiana
13. Mellowdrome—Asheville, North Carolina
14. The Velodrome at Bloomer Park—Rochester Hills, Michigan
15. National Sports Center Velodrome—Blaine, Minnesota
16. New England Velodrome—Londonberry, New Hampshire
17. San Diego Velodrome—San Diego, California
18. United States Olympic Training Center Velodrome—Colorado Springs, Colorado
19. Superdome—Frisco, Texas
20. Washington Park Velodrome—Kenosha, Wisconsin
21. Penrose Park Velodrome—St. Louis, Missouri
22. Idaho Velodrome and Cycling Park—Eagle, Idaho

Road Racing

Within road racing are four formats: road races, criteriums, time trials (individual or team), and stage races. Each format tends to attract different athletes, depending on their strengths and weaknesses. Teamwork and tactics also play a big part in road racing, and learning how to work together during a race is an important lesson in trust and communication.

Road races vary in length depending on your racing category and gender. Category 4 and 5 races are generally 30 to 40 miles long, while the more elite races (category 1 and 2) can range from 60 to 80 miles. Professional racers may ride more than 120 miles in a stage race. A criterium (or crit) is a multilap race that takes place on a closed circuit with a circumference of roughly 1 to 2 miles. The duration of a criterium depends on your racing category, but it generally ranges between 30 minutes to an hour. Criteriums are best suited for sprinters and racers who can produce large bursts of energy in a short time. Time trials can be done either individually or as a team and are individually timed events. In a team time trial, teammates learn to work together in a well-choreographed pace line. Using the principle of drafting, a team becomes greater than the sum of its parts. Both individual and team time trialing require the ability to hold a sustained effort over the course of the time trial. This is a different type of racing because you are not relying on short bursts of energy but rather a smooth consistent effort over time.

Whether you are a climber, sprinter, or time trialer, learning to use your strengths to your advantage is a huge part of learning how to race. In addition, learning to have confidence in your abilities is often the hardest lesson to learn in racing (and in life).

Mountain Bike Racing

Within mountain bike racing are two basic formats: cross-country or ultraendurance racing and gravity racing. Cross-country and ultraendurance racing rely heavily on long endurance fitness as well as good bike-handling skills. A typical cross-country course is primarily composed of a single track but may also include sections of gravel road or pavement and will vary in degree of technicality depending on the terrain. Variation in terrain will also determine the length of the course; however, most cross-country races range between one and a half to three hours depending on the racing category. In recent years, **short-track racing** (a multilap race that is relatively short and intense in comparison to the classic cross-country format) has also increased in popularity; it is similar to a criterium.

Endurance events such as 24-hour racing and 100-milers have created a large following within the mountain bike community and continue to grow in popularity. Laird Knight, father of 24-hour racing, held the first 24-hour race in 1992 and since then has become a celebrated icon in the mountain biking world. Six-time 24-hour solo world champion Chris Eatough (of the Trek Racing Co-op) gives an overview of 24-hour racing and provides insight into why this racing format is such a rewarding experience for those who participate:

> Most people that enter a 24-hour mountain bike race do so as part of a relay team, usually with three others as teammates. This relay format was created as a way to bring a rewarding team experience to mountain biking, which is usually an individual sport. The four teammates take turns riding a lap of an off-road course, usually around 10 miles long. This makes the 24-hour duration

Kid's-Eye View

Bike Racing

For a young person with an interest in bike racing, collegiate cycling clubs are an excellent way to make friends and learn the ins and outs of bike racing in a supportive environment. Collegiate cycling clubs are well known for their strong team camaraderie and school pride, creating a welcoming environment for even the newest of racers. As a club sport, collegiate bike racing is open to anyone interested in racing, and there are a variety of racing categories to accommodate each person's abilities. Collegiate cycling has also become quite competitive at the elite level and has served to jump-start the careers of many professional road cyclists and mountain bikers. From the novice racer to the aspiring professional cyclist, collegiate racing is a unique opportunity to experience a healthy balance of athletic competition and good college fun. For information on high school racing, visit www.norcalmtb.org.

much more reasonable, since each person "only" rides an average of 6 hours and can rest in between their laps. The exciting aspect of being immersed in an event all through the day and all through the night is quite unique, and the rider that is lucky enough to be on course for the morning lap when the sun rises is always treated to an amazing feeling of warmth and energy, no matter how much fatigue and discomfort came before.

One of the best lessons learned from the team relay format is the importance of being a dependable teammate and friend. This is the key to the number one rule of team relay racing: always be there when it's your turn to race! When your teammate comes in from a difficult and challenging lap, they are ready to pass the baton to you so that you can head out for your own portion of the team adventure, and keep the momentum going. Heaven forbid if the tired rider finds no teammate to take over, destroying trust and morale instantly.

However, a team that works well together and races around the clock will have a lasting bond forever. As long as each team member gives their best effort, is present for transitions, and is able to help out teammates and empathize if they struggle, the friendship and camaraderie will be stronger than ever. As tough as 24-hour mountain bike team relay races are, racers are often excitedly planning the next one with their friends before the bikes are even cleaned off from the one they just finished.

Then there are the people that choose to enter 24-hour mountain bike races by themselves in the solo category. This is not recommended for young people, since the duration, distance, and exertion is extreme. In mountain biking, it's the equivalent of climbing Mount Everest. It could be considered something for them to look forward and aspire to in the future if they find that they like the sport so much that they are ready for the ultimate mountain bike endurance challenge.

Following in the wake of 24-hour racing, 100-milers have also become popular among mountain bike racers, and attendance continues to grow. As the name suggests, these races are 100 miles of mountain bike racing. The course is usually one complete loop composed of single track, gravel roads, and pavement. The 2008 National Ultra-Endurance series champion Jeff Schalk (of the Trek Racing Co-op) reflects on ultraendurance racing and the lessons he has learned:

> Ultraendurance races are very grueling events that require many of the same keys that are necessary for success in life, including preparation, precise execution, and persistent focus. The demands of long racing require that the training leading up to the event be very thorough and exhaustive. This also includes paying very close attention to the bike preparation, making sure that as much is done ahead of time as possible so that potential mechanical issues are prevented. Execution of the race must be very precise, almost to the extent that you treat your body as a machine. This includes systematically ingesting fluids and food so that your body is fueled seamlessly, as well as paying close attention to your exertion level so that you don't blow up and fall apart late in the race. Most important, you must constantly focus. A lot of things can go wrong mechanically during a long event, and your mind may often tell you that you should stop because you are too close to your limits. Through such trials, belief in your abilities, confidence in your experience and preparation, and willingness to never give up are critical traits. For all these reasons, success in ultraendurance racing can be very rewarding.

Gravity Events

Gravity events are individually timed, downhill races that require a high level of skill, speed, and mental toughness. The three basic formats in gravity racing include downhill, dual slalom, and four-cross. Downhill racing is an individually timed event that takes place on trails that are far more technical and steep than your basic cross-country trail (figure 9.4). Dual slalom is very similar to dual slalom skiing, with two riders competing on a sweeping course. A dual slalom course is different from a downhill course: it takes place on hard packed dirt where there are no obstacles such as roots and rocks. Four-cross is fairly similar to BMX racing; however, it is much shorter, and there are only four competitors on the course at one time.

For all gravity events it is imperative to wear the proper protection as well as ride the appropriate bike. Protective wear includes a chest and back plate and a full-faced helmet, as well as arm, knee, and shin guards. Bikes used in gravity events have much more suspension than the basic cross-country bike. A cross-country bike is not built to absorb the shock of a large jump or drop and should not be used for any of the gravity events mentioned here.

Cyclocross Racing

Cyclocross racing originated in France in the early 1900s as a form of winter cross training for elite cyclists. Eventually it blossomed into its own form of racing and continues to be held during the wet, cold months of fall and winter. Something about racing in miserable weather conditions has attracted a devout following of racers and spectators, creating a rather jovial scene against a cold, bleak backdrop of snow and rain.

A typical cyclocross course is a closed circuit of roughly 1.5 to 2 miles that includes a number of obstacles that require continuous mounting and dismounting

Figure 9.4 Downhill mountain bike racing requires skill, concentration, and a dash of daring. Anna Kelso shows all three as she barrels downhill.

from the bike. In many ways, it is the steeplechase of bike racing. Cyclocross races are similar to criteriums; they are short, intense races that usually last 40 to 60 minutes. Some racers are skilled enough to **bunny hop** (jump over hazards by lifting up and pulling the bike with them) their bikes over the barriers; however, most people dismount and run with their bikes. It is for this reason that many cyclocross racers incorporate running into their training regimen.

Cyclocross racing is especially popular in Belgium, drawing large boisterous crowds of all ages. In recent years, cyclocross racing has gained popularity in the United States, and the number of racers and spectators continues to grow each year. Cyclocross racing is especially spectator friendly and is a great way to stay in shape during the winter months.

CONCLUSION

Whether you end up racing in the Tour de France or riding around on a trail near your house every weekend, bicycling is a great way to stay in shape and get outdoors. From group rides and mountain biking to the huge variety of bike racing events, there is a place in cycling for everyone.

READY TO RIDE

Whether you're getting on your bike after a long hiatus or getting on for the first time since childhood, you should approach the experience with thought and planning. For the experience to be enjoyable and free of injury, it's important to start with the right bike, to exercise prudence in planning the initial outings, and to take good care of the motor, your body, with proper fuel and maintenance. This chapter is devoted to a discussion of the full body–bicycle experience, including tips on developing and maintaining speed and endurance, tactics for staying injury free, and nutrition advice for weight loss and optimal performance.

GET ON YOUR BIKE

Regular exercise is the key to good fitness. It is critical for beginner cyclists to build up to longer rides and allow time for rest and recovery. Start by riding every other day, gradually increasing to five or six days a week. A novice may try to ride two to five miles per day, gradually increasing mileage as conditioning allows.

If you get serious about bike riding, you will pay more attention to your personal fitness and nutrition. How fast and how long you can ride are a product of the conditioning you gain from riding and proper nutrition. Trained riders can more easily handle higher-intensity and longer-duration rides. Your personal fitness goals will dictate your training regimen. Always consult a physician before beginning any training or fitness program.

If you haven't been riding or commuting all winter, your first ride of the season should be short so that you can assess your physical strength and the condition of your bike. You may discover that there are some things you overlooked or forgot that you will want to change or correct for your next outing.

CADENCE AND SPINNING

Cadence, the rate of pedaling, is measured in revolutions per minute (rpm) of one foot. Cadence is critical because it affects your comfort, speed, and endurance on the bike as well as the long-term health of the cartilage, tendons, and ligaments of your knees. In theory, the different gears on your bike allow you to pedal at a constant pace, applying the same amount of force regardless of terrain. While there are other concerns, you should always try to use your gears to maintain a comfortable and steady cadence. Spinning (the rate at which you pedal) at a cadence of 65 to 95 rpm, even up hills, will allow you to ride stronger for a longer period of time. To find your approximate cadence, count the number of times your pedals make one complete revolution in 15 seconds and multiply that number by four. Some bike computers display a cadence measurement.

To minimize wear and tear on your knees, when you start out on a ride, spin gently for the first 10 to 15 minutes to warm up. Also avoid grinding up hills in an uncomfortably high gear. On climbs, when you notice your cadence dropping and your effort per pedal stroke increasing, shift to an easier gear and alternate between standing on the pedals and sitting down. When you stand, shift to a slightly harder (higher) gear.

GEARING

Bicyclists use different gear combinations depending on their desired speed, cadence, and terrain (whether they are going uphill, downhill, or on flat ground). Using a multigeared bike is similar to using a standard transmission on a car. In your car, you shift gears to get the most out of the engine. On a bicycle, you are the engine, and you should use the gears to allow you to pedal with maximum efficiency and minimal strain on the engine (particularly your knees).

If you are a casual cyclist or new to the sport, be conscious of the danger of pedaling in an unnecessarily hard gear and not shifting frequently enough. It is better for your knees, lungs, circulation, and muscle development to use low gears. Proper gearing is key to keeping your cadence between 65 and 95 rpm. Taking advantage of your gears to pedal at these high cadences will allow you to ride longer and help prevent knee strain.

STOP AND GO RIDING

If you find yourself in traffic with a lot of traffic lights, try to pace yourself so you miss the red lights. If you have to stop, downshift so you will not have to start from a high gear. If you are using toe clips or clipless pedals (clipless pedals release when the rider twists her foot to the side), unclip before you have to stop, and wait until you are through the intersection to click in. It is always better to be safe than sorry; every cyclist has a story about falling over because she did not unclip soon enough.

RIDING POSITION

Once your cadence is steady and you ride longer, you may realize other parts of your body, such as neck, hands, and back, get fatigued. Maintain your comfort by changing hand positions on your handlebars often. Keep your elbows and shoulders relaxed; do neck and shoulder stretches throughout the ride. Take a few deep, relaxing breaths and enjoy the scenery around you. If your body stiffens up, try pedaling while standing for 15 seconds. If you are really sore, dismount and take a short break.

BIKE FIT, REVISITED

There are many types of bikes, and each type has various sizes and submeasurements that can affect your comfort. A well-fitted bike is essential for your comfort, for peddling efficiency, and for avoiding injury. Bike fit starts with having the right size bicycle frame and then fine-tuning the crank length, saddle height and position, handlebars, and stem height and length to your body.

The fit of the bike can make or break comfort on longer rides. Improper seat positioning can result in inefficient pedaling and strain on the knees. A saddle that is too high may cause pain in the back of the knee; one that is too low often produces pain in the front of the knee. The length of your top tube combined with the stem height and length dictate how far you are stretched out to reach the handlebars. Your arms should be slightly bent to provide cushion from road shock; your hands should comfortably grasp the handlebar and easily reach the brakes. If you experience pain or discomfort in your back, neck, or arms, readjust the stem or handlebar to find a better, more comfortable position. Though it might take some time to find the proper adjustments, your ride should be comfortable (figure 10.1).

Figure 10.1 When your bike is fitted to your body, you can ride more comfortably, pedal more efficiently, and avoid strains and injuries.

YOUR FEET AND SHOES

The most important feature of footwear for cycling is a stiff sole. Stiff, inflexible soles deliver more of your energy to the pedal. Toe clips or cleated shoes with step-in pedals help increase your pedaling efficiency and prevent your feet from slipping off the pedals when accelerating or braking. To become comfortable with toe straps or clips, keep them loose until you are accustomed to getting your feet in and out of them.

The most efficient pedal system available today is the clipless pedal. Available in a variety of designs, clipless pedals allow more power transfer to the cranks, encouraging a supple, efficient pedal stroke. Because your feet are locked into your pedal, you are able to get more power from your upstroke. Clipless pedals release when the rider twists her foot to the side. They work much the same way as the bindings on a pair of downhill skis.

INCREASING THE EFFICIENCY OF THE BICYCLE ENGINE

Heart rate is one of the best measures of performance level and exertion when exercising. It is generally recommended that you sustain your target heart rate for 20 to 30 minutes of constant physical activity to increase your personal aerobic fitness level. Your target heart rate is 65 to 85 percent of your maximum heart rate. Your maximum heart rate can be determined by this formula:

$$208 - (0.7 \times age)$$

For example, if you are a 30-year-old male, your maximum heart rate is 208 minus (0.7×30), or 187 beats per minute. Your target heart rate would be 65 to 85 percent of this maximum, or approximately 122 to 159 beats per minute.

A more accurate method for determining your target heart rate is the Karvonen method, which takes your current fitness level into account. To calculate your target heart rate using the Karvonen method, you need to know your maximum heart rate and your resting heart rate. Count your pulse for 10 seconds first thing in the morning, and then multiply it by 6 to determine your resting heart rate. To continue the example above, let's say the 30-year-old male counts 12 heart beats in 10 seconds. His resting heart rate is $12 \times 6 = 72$ beats per minute. We already know his maximum heart rate is 187. The equation for finding his target heart rate using the Karvonen method is

$$\text{target heart rate} = (\text{maximum heart rate} - \text{resting heart rate}) \times \text{percent intensity} + \text{resting heart rate.}$$

If the 30-year-old male wants to exercise at an intensity of 65 percent of his maximum heart rate, his target heart rate would be

$$\text{target heart rate} = (187 - 72) \times 0.65 + 72$$

$$\text{target heart rate} = 115 \times 0.65 + 72$$

$$\text{target heart rate} = 75 + 72$$

$$\text{target heart rate} = 147$$

At 85 percent intensity, his target heart rate would be

$$\text{target heart rate} = (187 - 72) \times 0.85 + 72$$

$$\text{target heart rate} = 115 \times 0.85 + 72$$

$$\text{target heart rate} = 98 + 72$$

$$\text{target heart rate} = 170$$

So, to exercise at 65 to 85 percent intensity, the 30-year-old male's target heart rate range is 147 to 170 beats per minute.

This is a quick way to measure your heart rate, but it is not as accurate as other measures, such as the heart rate monitors that are now a part of high-end bicycle computers. Using a heart rate monitor will give you a much better measure of your peak heart rate. Another easy way to know if you are working at your target heart rate is this rule of thumb: If you can sing, you haven't reached your target. If you can talk, and not sing, you have achieved it. If you can't talk without gasping, you're working a bit too hard.

Achieving and maintaining your target heart rate are facilitated by efficient use of the gearing on your bicycle.

SETTING GOALS FOR SADDLE TIME

Beginners should start small and build gradually. You do not have to go farther or harder every time you ride. Set your goals based on your motivations for riding: weight loss, transportation, touring, competitive racing, or general fitness.

If you are the average healthy couch potato and want to prepare to ride a century (a 100-mile bike ride), you probably need 10 to 12 weeks to train. Table 10.1 shows how to train for a century in 10 weeks. This plan details riding every day each week except for one and alternating between easy, normal, and brisk rides. For example, on day 1 of week 1, you would ride 6 miles at an easy pace. This time period is supported by organizations hosting charity functions such as century rides and marathons. New riders should not expect to be fast on such long rides, but they will be able to finish them. This recommendation of 10 to 12 weeks for preparation also assumes that the rider, although inactive, is in general good health (no high blood pressure, heart issues, diabetes, and so on). Charity groups, such as the Multiple Sclerosis Society and the American Diabetes Association, are great organizations to start with when you are trying to get fit and train to ride a century. These organizations usually have a coach who works with riders, organizes rides, and provides a basic riding schedule. These programs also allow new riders to meet and ride with others for motivation. Completing the final event is significant; riders feel a wonderful sense of accomplishment.

If your goal is to increase your ability to ride comfortably farther and longer, then you will need to prepare for this. Training sounds hard, but it can be fun. The best way to train is to have a plan, work the plan, and keep track of your progress. The two things you are trying to accomplish are building mileage and increasing endurance.

Table 10.1   Mileage Training Chart

Week	Day 1	Day 2	Day 3	Day 4	Day 5	Day 6	Day 7	Total
Pace	Easy	Norm	Brisk	—	Norm	Norm	Norm	
1	6	10	12	0	10	30	9	77
2	7	11	13	0	11	34	10	86
3	8	13	15	0	13	38	11	98
4	8	14	17	0	14	42	13	108
5	9	15	19	0	15	47	14	119
6	11	15	21	0	15	53	16	131
7	12	15	24	0	15	59	18	143
8	13	15	25	0	15	65	20	153
9	15	15	25	0	15	65	20	155
10	15	15	25	0	10	5	100	170

BUILDING MILEAGE

Plan to increase your total weekly mileage by no more than 10 to 12 percent each week. Try to ride four to six days per week—bicycle commuting is a great way to achieve this goal. Try to get in a long ride on the weekend. Plan a combination of easy, normal (your usual speed), and brisk rides each week. Limit stops to 5 to 10 minutes; for rides more than 75 miles long, it is recommended that you take one 5-minute stop every hour.

MASSAGE AND BODY-BASED HEALING

Professional athletes are massaged almost every day, and many keep limber by adding yoga or other body-based practices to supplement their bike workouts. Consider treating yourself sometime, such as during or after a hard multiday ride. If you ride with friends, give each other 15-minute neck and back rubs after a long day of riding. Other helpful recovery tools are ice baths, hot tubs, and saunas. Yoga, relaxation with deep breathing, and meditation can help keep your mind and body limber and prevent injury.

FITNESS THROUGH CYCLING

Fitness—getting fit and maintaining it—is critical for any bicyclist. Some say that bicycling is all legs and lungs. If you subscribe to this theory, make sure you take care of both by avoiding cigarettes and keeping your legs limber and healthy. Other body-based discipline is also important to successful cyclists. The average bicyclist burns at least 400 calories an hour and requires calories just to keep pedaling, so eating is a cyclist's second-favorite activity. Keeping your back, neck, and arms limber is also important for successful cyclists. Strong abdominal and core muscles are key to endurance, good climbing, and out-of-saddle sprinting.

Bicycling strengthens your heart, helps reduce blood pressure, increases lung efficiency, and keeps your energy level up all day. In addition, bicycling burns calories, so combining a sensible diet with bicycling is a terrific way to lose weight and get fit.

Losing weight through any form of exercise is accomplished through two processes. First, exercise burns calories, so any time you exceed your usual activities, you burn more calories. If you maintain your usual caloric intake, you will slowly lose weight. Second, exercise builds muscles, and muscles themselves burn additional calories all day long. So exercise, either alone or in combination with a reduced-calorie diet, will not only improve fitness but also lower your weight. There's just one caveat: Muscle weighs more than fat, so your weight loss may not be as evident on the scale as it is in your appearance.

The exact number of calories burned depends on the energy you expend. For example, table 10.2 shows that the faster you pedal, the more calories you burn. Diet plus biking can be a formula for a healthy future with a stronger heart, lower blood pressure, and increased energy level. You will also be able to ride farther and faster than you ever thought possible.

Regardless of your reasons for improving your fitness, it is always important to have goals. Whether your goal is to finish a century in six hours, lose weight, or simply beat your friends to the top of a climb, keep your goals realistic. Once you reach your goal, set a new one for the next week, month, or following year.

Table 10.2   Calories Burned by Bicycling

Miles per hour	Calories per hour
6	240-300
8	300-360
10	360-420
11	420-480
12	480-600
13	600-660

STRETCHING

Just as good bicycle handling reduces the potential for crashes, a few basic warm-up and stretching exercises before you ride can dramatically reduce the potential for injury to vital muscles. Warm-ups and stretching also increase blood supply to the muscles, carrying the oxygen and nutrients muscles need. Muscles have inter-crossed fibers that stick together when idle. You need to loosen them before you ride so that muscle fibers do not tear and cause injury.

Ease into warm-ups and stretches. Stretch slowly at first. If pain occurs when stretching, decrease the intensity or the stretch.

Take it easy for the first 5 to 10 minutes of riding. This gives your heart time to pump blood to the muscles and for the muscles to fully warm up. Near the end of your ride, ease off and cycle more gently for 5 or 10 minutes to cool down. When you get off the bike, stretch a bit to help relax your muscles.

Neck and Shoulders

Loosen neck muscles by rolling your head first one way then the other (see figure 10.2a). Raise your shoulders toward your ears, hold briefly, then relax. This will help to loosen shoulder muscles.

Quadriceps and Lower Back

Sit on the floor. Lift your buttocks off the floor and twist your lower back (figure 10.2b). Hold for 10 seconds and repeat for the other side. This helps stretch the muscles on top of your thighs and in your lower back.

PREVENTING INJURIES

For maximum prevention of injury, lightly stretch before your ride, and then, for 5 to 10 minutes, ride slowly at a low gear so your pedals spin quickly without putting pressure on your knees or ankles. At this point, get off your bike and stretch again before mounting for your ride. Stretch one last time after completing your ride.

Hamstrings

Lower back pain often comes from tight, tensed hamstrings. Make your ride more comfortable by stretching to warm up these vital muscles. Sit on the floor with your legs out straight in front of your body. Draw one leg up close to the body with the foot placed against the other leg as shown in figure 10.2c. Stretch your arms forward as far as possible to the foot of the outstretched leg. Hold this position for 10 seconds and repeat for the other leg. Do not bounce.

Calf and Achilles Tendon

Your legs are a very important part of your bicycle's engine. Warm up the Achilles tendons and calves by stretching the back of each leg. Grab the back of a chair, a wall, or a tree. Bend one knee, stretching the other leg (see figure 10.2d). Hold for 15 seconds, and then repeat for the other leg.

NUTRITION AND HYDRATION

Riding a bicycle is physically demanding, especially at high speeds or over long distances. If you plan on riding for more than 30 minutes, you should bring along food and something to drink. The traditional wisdom on nutrition and hydration still holds true: Eat before you are hungry, and drink before you are thirsty.

The exertion of bicycling will probably cause you to perspire more heavily than you normally do. You may not notice how much moisture you are losing because the air flowing over your body will often dry the perspiration on your skin. Dehydration is a serious condition that can decrease your performance and, in extreme cases, be life threatening. As a general rule, plan to drink one 20-ounce bottle of water per hour. Take a generous swig of water every 10 to 15 minutes.

Drink more than this the day before a long ride or on extremely hot days. If you show any symptoms of dehydration (see the sidebar), stop riding immediately and rest. Find shade if it is sunny and hot, or go indoors, if possible. Drink as much water as you can during this rest period, and monitor how you feel before getting back on your bike to ride home. After the ride, be sure to keep drinking water the next couple of hours because the rehydration process depends on a continuous flow of water through the body.

You can also incorporate sport drinks into your hydration plans. These drinks can greatly improve your riding enjoyment because they contain carbohydrate and other nutrients that will help sustain your body and speed its recovery following a challenging ride.

Fuel the Machine

There are two types of food that are critical for cycling: food you eat while on the bike and food you eat while off the bike.

On-the-bike foods, such as bananas (or other fresh or dried fruit) and energy bars and gels, contain simple carbohydrate (also called sugar) that can quickly be converted for use as energy by your body. Found in fruits and vegetables, simple carbohydrate provides quick energy and is not stored by the body to maintain

a

b

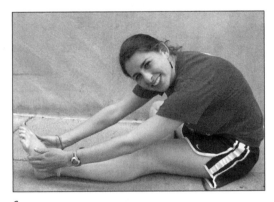

c

d

Figure 10.2 *(a)* Your neck and shoulders can really stiffen up while riding; this is a great stretch for cyclists. *(b)* Lower back pain can be prevented with this simple warm-up. *(c)* Keeping your legs limber is a key part of enjoying your ride. *(d)* This stretch helps prevent cramping, a debilitating condition all cyclists face at one point or another.

SYMPTOMS OF DEHYDRATION

If you feel thirsty, chances are you are already beginning to dehydrate. Symptoms of dehydration include the following:

- Dull headache
- Muscle cramping
- Brightly colored or dark urine
- Dry lips and tongue
- Cessation of perspiration during physical activity
- Apathy and lack of energy

energy levels. Eating while riding will enhance your energy level throughout your ride and the rest of the day.

Off-the-bike foods that help store energy for your ride generally consist of complex carbohydrate (also called starches). Grains, pastas, breads, cereals, and potatoes are great sources of complex carbohydrate. These provide long-term energy to adequately fuel you through rides. For an added bonus, do yourself a favor and eat carbohydrate that is high in fiber. Foods like brown rice, whole wheat pasta, and bran cereal are great sources of fiber and carbohydrate. Fiber makes you feel full faster and lowers the number of calories you absorb from food.

Always try to keep fat, sugar, and salt to a minimum. Lean meat, fish, beans, and low-fat dairy products help round out a healthful diet. Protein and carbohydrate generally work well when eaten in combination. This is a good all-around diet, but if you are not exercising regularly you should limit the amount of complex carbohydrate you eat.

Recovery is an important aspect of bike riding. If you are training for a century or competitive event, resting and eating well after riding is as important as the work you do on your bike. A long or hard workout can affect your metabolism for 24 hours or more.

Here are some tips to help you recover properly after a long ride:

- Save an energy bar for the last few miles of your ride or for a postride snack.
- Pick up something extra to drink while you cool down from your ride.
- Try to avoid a fatty meal that will take a lot of time and energy to digest.

The more you ride, the more you will understand how your body works and what you need to do to keep it in top form. There are many books dedicated to sport nutrition and training, including training for cycling events. From *The Lance Armstrong Performance Program* by Lance Armstrong and Chris Carmichael to *The Cyclist's Training Bible* by Joe Friel, there are books to cover every kind of higher-level training you might be interested in.

Kid's-Eye View

Ready to Ride

Here are some tips to get children ready to ride. Children should

- practice balancing in an open field or vacant parking lot;
- practice riding in circles as well as in a straight line;
- learn how to use the brakes and how to skid the rear wheel;
- ride straight and look back at you without swerving;
- scan for traffic in front of them as well as behind before signaling; and
- learn the signals for a right turn, left turn, and a stop, as well as when to use these signals.

Once they've mastered these skills, take them on a neighborhood ride. Plan a ride with your child around your neighborhood and discuss possible dangers. Include children in the planning of the ride, and then allow them to lead. You'll be happy with how much they have learned!

Preparing for an Event

Eating and drinking properly before the start of a cross-state ride or even a one-day city tour is also important. You should drink additional fluids starting two days before the event. The night before the event, consume additional carbohydrate in anticipation of your day on the bike. A meal that includes a significant portion of rice or pasta can help provide your body with the energy it will need. Avoid fatty foods the morning of the event because these are hard to digest and may slow down your body's energy system. Cereal, fruit, juice, and toast with jam will give you the energy to start the day strong. You may want to have an energy bar as well.

Remember the general rule: Eat before you are hungry and drink before you are thirsty. Eat and drink at a slow, steady pace while bicycling. Plan when and what you will consume, and you will find that you will enjoy the ride much more.

Alcohol

Prolonged consumption of alcohol will increase the amount of time it takes your muscles to recover from a ride and reduce your endurance. One of the most noticeable physical effects of too much alcohol consumption will be your body's reduced ability to metabolize fat. Instead of shedding excess fat cells, your body will be counteracting your efforts and become more efficient at fat storage. Your body will see reduced gains from your cycling efforts. While it is OK to have a few drinks per week, you should avoid drinking beer or other alcohol daily. In addition, your body uses water to metabolize alcohol into sugar, so it dehydrates you as well as increasing the amount of calories you consume.

TWO TIPS TO GET LEANER AND STRONGER

1. Refuel fast. Following a hard ride, your glycogen stores are tapped. Refill them quickly by chugging a recovery drink that contains both carbohydrate and protein to refuel and repair your muscles. This should be done within 30 minutes of the end of your ride. By sensibly refueling right away, you prevent a ravenous, postride, fast-food binge later on, and you will get fit faster.

2. Pedal just 1 mph faster. Ride an hour at 13 mph, and you will burn about 545 calories. Pick up the pace to 14 mph to burn 680 calories. If you ride most days of the week, that slight change can add (or subtract) up to 10 pounds a year from your body weight.

CONCLUSION

The staff at the League of American Bicyclists hopes you have discovered or rediscovered bicycling as a result of reading this book. If your next step is becoming a cycling enthusiast, trying a cross-state, multiday ride, or leaving the car in the garage while going for a few groceries, we have accomplished our mission.

The joys of cycling are many for every cyclist. We hope they will be discovered by all types of riders, young and old, whether or not you are completely new to the notion of riding for pleasure, transportation, or fitness. And finally, as you drive down the road, perhaps your new perspective on cyclists will inspire you to share the roads generously, be patient, and wave in acknowledgment to any two-wheeled, motor-free vehicles with whom you happen to be sharing your route.

If you'd like to find more resources for cyclists in your area, including cycling instructors, local cycling clubs and advocacy groups, and much more, go to our Web site at www.bikeleague.org. Click Find It and enter your zip code, and all the resources in your area will be at your fingertips. You can also contact the league at Bikeleague@bikeleague.org with any questions.

PARTS OF THE BICYCLE

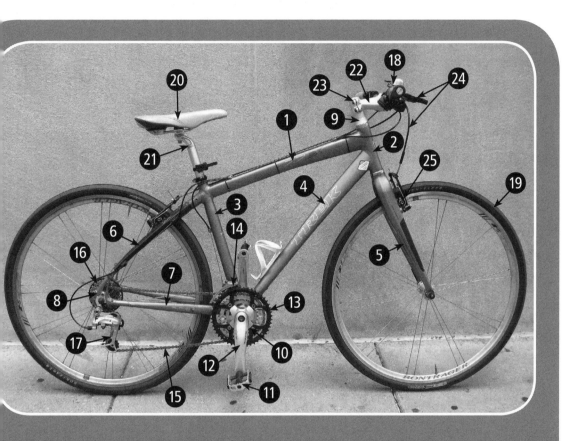

FRAME
1. Top tube
2. Head tube
3. Seat tube
4. Down tube
5. Fork
6. Seat stays
7. Chain stays
8. Dropouts
9. Headset
10. Bottom bracket

DRIVE TRAIN
11. Pedal
12. Cranks
13. Chainrings
14. Front derailleur
15. Chain
16. Cassette
17. Rear derailleur
18. Shifters and cables
19. Wheel—hub, spokes, rim, tire, rim strip, tube, valve

OTHER COMPONENTS
20. Saddle
21. Seat post
22. Handlebar
23. Handlebar stem
24. Brake lever and cables
25. Brakes

eague of American Bicyclists, 2011, *Smart cycling: Promoting safety, fun, fitness, and the environment* (Champaign, IL: Human s).

TOP 13 BICYCLE FRIENDLY COMMUNITIES IN THE UNITED STATES

The league is changing the look of America with the Bicycle Friendly State, Bicycle Friendly Community, and Bicycle Friendly Business programs. These programs offer technical assistance from league staff, an in-depth application that gives participants an opportunity to self-evaluate, and feedback to all applicants—recognized or not. The program, launched in 2003 and sponsored generously by Bikes Belong and Trek's One World Two Wheels program, encourages states, communities, and businesses to provide better facilities, encouragement activities, infrastructure, and education for cyclists and publicly rewards them for doing so.

BOULDER, COLORADO

Boulder, Colorado, received the league's platinum-level Bicycle Friendly Community (BFC) designation in 2008, moving up from their 2004 gold-level BFC designation. Boulder's bicycle network and the services for cyclists are some of the most impressive in the nation. The city employs a **complete streets** approach (an urban planning policy focusing on designing and operating roadways to enable safe, attractive, and comfortable access and travel for all users) when considering major transportation facility enhancements and maintains their bikeways to a high level in transportation standards. Transportation systems cohere to making biking and walking the more accessible and effortless choice. Boulder's multimodal corridors are designed to provide citizens with an easy choice and transition between pedestrian, bike, bus, and automobile connections. The expansive bike network has even led local real estate agents to show homes by bike in an effort to highlight the location's proximity to the network. In 2009, the city and its partners added 2 new underpasses, raising the count to 76 underpasses on the multiuse pathway system. To help bike commuters navigate the city's 380-mile network of bike facilities and trails, the city hosts GOBikeBoulder.net. The site helps cyclists coordinate routes, terrain, and traffic by offering information on turn-by-turn biking routes, miles traveled, and calories burned, as well as the amounts of CO_2 and gas saved by not driving.

DAVIS, CALIFORNIA

Bicycling is embedded into Davis' identity—so much so that the city's logo is a bike. Davis has been the pioneer city for innovative ways to accommodate and welcome cyclists for the last 40 years. Before there were local, state, or national guidelines, the city researched and developed its own set and built a great bicycle-friendly community. It was the first city to receive the platinum-level BFC designation. When the California Department of Transportation (CALTRANS) began formulating its own guidelines a number of years later, much of their work was loosely based on what Davis had developed. And when national guidelines were developed, much of the work was based on what CALTRANS had done—an amazing 40-year progression that spread from Davis to communities throughout the country. The city worked to get state laws changed to favor bicycling, and Davis continues to labor for a more bike-friendly community and state. Davis' population explosion, from 6,000 residents to 60,000, may be one consequence of the place of bicycling at the core of the city's comprehensive plan—there are more bikes in Davis than there are cars! Davis has bike lanes on approximately 95 percent of all its arterial and collector streets. The city has 27 different grade separations for bicycles and pedestrians. In the last 10 years alone, the city has spent more than $14 million on bicycle projects.

PORTLAND, OREGON

Bicycle provisions and promotion are integrated into almost every action taken by the city of Portland, from the mayor's office to maintenance crews on the streets. Portland has a seamless and varied bicycle network that connects the whole city and has proven successful in increasing ridership. Portland has dramatically increased its bicycle use and has developed a strong bicycle culture; all types of cyclists can find limitless opportunities to enjoy riding a bicycle. Annually there are an estimated 2,100 rides, races, and other events held to encourage cyclists—an average of 6 per day—and they draw more than 40,000 participants. Portland's increased ridership comes with an improved focus on safety through a Share the Road ticket diversion program, newly installed side underrun guards on all city trucks, and an Eye to Eye cyclist visibility campaign. The Bicycle Transportation Alliance offers one of the nation's leading Safe Routes to School programs. The Community Cycling Center also offers an exciting Create a Commuter program that provides low-income adults with a fully outfitted commuter bike, requisite commuting gear, and bike safety training. In Portland, 60 percent of the downtown police officers are on bikes.

CORVALLIS, OREGON

Corvallis has a 22 percent bicycle **mode share** (the percentage share that a particular type of transportation mode has in relation to other modes), bike lanes on 97 percent of arterial streets, and bicycle education and encouragement programs like week-long bicycle training for fifth graders and bicycle diversion programs that allow cited bicyclists to participate in an education program in lieu of a ticket. The city's police department participates at every Bicycle Commission meeting, and the city has developed many bicycle-related educational materials that are available to the public. One of the department's performance measures is the number of bicycle or skateboard citations. Based on the number of citations, the community puts problem locations on the Directed Patrol lists. The Bicycle and Pedestrian Advisory Commission has a public comment period at all meetings, and the town's Web site encourages comments to staff or elected officials. To encourage riding, the city sponsors the August in Motion initiative and Get There Another Way Week (also supported by Oregon State University and other local employers). The Intermodal Transit Mall with bike racks and bike storage lockers is a model for other communities to consider.

EUGENE, OREGON

Eugene has a 7 percent bicycle mode share, more than 10 times the national average. This high rate of ridership can be attributed to a well-connected on- and off-street bicycle network, supportive city policies, and an engaged bicycle advocacy community. Eugene's commitment to providing facilities and support for bicycling has resulted in greater community livability for all residents. Destinations within the city have ample bike parking, the off-street path network is expanding yearly, and bike boulevards provide comfortable riding conditions for all types of bicyclists. Children in Eugene are exposed to bicycling early through a comprehensive Safe Routes to School program that advocates for and promotes the practice of safe bicycling as well as walking to and from schools. In addition to a great urban cycling network, Eugene's recreational cyclists can access the Pacific coast to the west and the Cascade Mountains to the east on low-traffic, bike-friendly, rural roads. City staff and local advocates encourage bicycling at events year round, including the annual Bike Day, the Eugene Walking and Biking Summit, monthly Breakfast at the Bridges events in the summer, and International Walk and Bike to School Day. The city of Eugene recently obtained a significant amount of federal stimulus dollars to allocate toward infrastructure and programmatic projects to increase local bicycle ridership.

FORT COLLINS, COLORADO

Fort Collins makes bike commuting easy with its integrated on- and off-street bicycle network and its informative Web site, www.fcgov.com/bicycling, complete with shared lane marking information, bike project updates, educational materials, events, and federal transportation updates. The city's flat terrain, 280-plus miles of wide bike lanes, and 30-plus miles of bike trails that follow the scenic Poudre River and Spring Creek make commuting a breeze. The surrounding vicinity offers incredible road biking, and there is also great mountain biking nearby.

JACKSON AND TETON COUNTY, WYOMING

Teton County voters overwhelmingly approved $6 million in an optional 1-cent sales tax for a pathway connection between Wilson and Jackson, Wyoming. Jackson has developed a Pathway Master Plan that outlines nonmotorized **mode-shift** (changing the form of transportation) goals, total number of paths, and a complete streets guide for Teton County. Friends of Pathways, the local nonprofit nonmotorized advocacy group, partners with the Wyoming Department of Transportation to organize Bike to Work events during June and partners with the Sheriff's Department to co-sponsor a Kid's Bike Rodeo. The city consistently parks more than 400 bicycles each Fourth of July during the Music in the Hole concert.

MADISON, WISCONSIN

Mayor Dave Cieslewicz formed the Platinum Biking City Planning Committee with the goal of becoming a platinum BFC. The committee's report, *Making Madison the Best Place in the Country to Bicycle,* was adopted by the city council in April of 2008. This report lays out an exciting future for cyclists in the city. "Objectives and Policies for the City of Madison," part of the plan, supports a flexible transportation system that provides alternative modes of travel to most destinations, minimizes conflicts among the different modes, and discourages single-occupant motor vehicle commuting. Bicycle infrastructure is included when constructing or reconstructing city streets, and there are requirements for bicycle traffic in all traffic control device designs. Almost all roadway projects funded with Surface Transportation Programs-Urban Program (STU) funding over the past 10 years have included bike lanes. Another impressive testament to cycling is the abundance of riders in the area who commute all year long, even through Wisconsin winters.

PALO ALTO, CALIFORNIA

Palo Alto's BFC status is not just about past efforts but is an integral part of the city's vision for a more sustainable transportation future in which residents choose alternatives to driving. Recent engineering improvements include their second bicycle boulevard, a 2.8-mile route that serves three schools and provides better connectivity to transit and major employment districts. A third boulevard is scheduled for 2010, enhancing links, safety, and signage along the last unimproved segment. The city also partners with the Palo Alto Unified School District and the Palo Alto Council of PTAs to provide an in-class traffic safety education program for kindergarten through sixth grade. Parent education is facilitated by PTA traffic safety representatives in each school.

SAN FRANCISCO, CALIFORNIA

The 2008 American Communities Survey tracked a 37-percent rise in bicycle commuting in San Francisco since 2000, and the 2000 Census showed that San Francisco has the highest percentage of residents who commute to work by bicycle among cities with a population of 500,000 or above in the United States. The Golden Gate Bridge has a path that is available for cyclists 24 hours a day, and the Bay Bridge will have a 15.5-foot wide bicycle and pedestrian path that will run along the eastbound deck of the 2-mile long structure. Bicycles are allowed on BART commuter rail, CALTRAIN commuter heavy rail, and on all ferries and bike-rack-equipped buses.

There is a bike shuttle across the Bay Bridge during rush hour. San Francisco promotes Bike Month, with as many as 35,000 people riding into San Francisco on Bike to Work Day. The San Francisco Police Department works with cyclists, helping with issues from safety to bicycle theft to injury collision reporting. The city has an excellent partnership with the San Francisco Bicycle Coalition (SFBC). Another excellent program is SFBC's education for various kinds of professional drivers including taxi, USPS, and other delivery drivers.

SEATTLE, WASHINGTON

Seattle's Bicycle Master Plan is one of the most progressive in the nation, with green bike lanes at a dozen locations, and the 3.6-mile Chief Sealth Trail made of recycled materials. The plan calls for a 455-mile network that would put 95 percent of Seattle residents within a quarter-mile of a bike facility. Each year, the program will target two of six city zones with a neighborhood-based bicycle encouragement and education campaign that seeks to increase bicycle ridership, trips, and safety. Residents will be able to request bicycle information kits that will include a bicycle map, safety information, and a calendar of community programming that will be personally delivered by the city's Bicycle Ambassadors, who will also lead neighborhood clinics and participate in special events such as low-cost helmet sales. SDOT officials also meet regularly with Seattle's Police Department Traffic Division to discuss problem locations and enforcement solutions.

STANFORD UNIVERSITY, CALIFORNIA

The daily on-campus population of more than 13,000 students, faculty, and staff at Stanford University needs to be able to move in a relatively confined space, and encouraging bicycle use is one of their means of doing so. One-third of Stanford's roadways have bike lanes. They have traffic circles to reduce conflict between pedestrians and cyclists, more than 50 bike lockers, and an estimated 175 bike racks throughout campus, bringing total bike parking to over 12,000. Lockers and showers are also available for commuting cyclists. Other encouragement efforts include valet bike parking at home football games and other events, and a $282 stipend for bike commuting to eligible members of the Commute Club. To encourage new students to ride, Stanford sponsors the Dormitory Road Show to discuss bike safety and encourage helmet use, in addition to giving out 2,500 bike lights and 200 helmets.

TUCSON AND EAST PIMA REGION, ARIZONA

Tucson's mayor and city council have passed a policy to include bike lanes on all new street construction, as well as on all reconstruction projects. A Bikeway Improvement Program and a Spot Bicycle/Pedestrian Improvements List have been implemented with the help of the Tucson-Pima County Bicycle Advisory Committee. Additionally, Tucson and Pima County's Safe Routes to Schools program held 74 rodeos and reached over 2,000 schoolchildren in 2009. The free bicycle safety classes continue to be popular, with over 600 participants attending Smart Cycling, Commuting, or Kids Safety classes.

GLOSSARY

avoidance weave—An avoidance maneuver that consists of a set of swooping turns executed to avoid a series of hazards.

barrel adjusters—Small mechanisms used for making minor adjustments on brake or shifter cables.

Bicycle Friendly Community—A designation of the League of American Bicyclists to recognize communities that have worked to create safe and welcoming places for cycling.

BMX—Bicycle motocross, which is stunt riding on rough ground or on an obstacle course.

bottom bracket—The part of the frame around which the pedal cranks revolve.

brake hood—Covering for the brake lever mechanism where you can rest your hands.

brake pads—The rubber parts of the brake that contact the rim of the wheel and provide stopping power.

bunny hop—A way to jump over hazards by lifting up and pulling your bike with you.

cadence—The rate of rotation of the pedals.

cassette—A cluster of gear sprockets and spacers.

century—A ride of 100 miles normally done in a day.

chainring—A front gear sprocket.

clipless pedals—A type of pedal that requires a shoe with a cleat, locking your shoe to the pedal and providing better pedaling efficiency.

coaster brakes—Brakes that use a mechanism inside the rear hub to stop the wheel from turning and require you to push backward on the pedals to stop.

cog—Popular term for a rear gear sprocket.

complete streets—Streets designed and operated to enable safe access for all users. Pedestrians, bicyclists, motorists, and public transportation users of all ages and abilities are able to safely move along and across a complete street.

crank—The arm that connects the pedal to the bottom bracket axle.

criteriums—Multilap races that take place on a closed circuit with a circumference of roughly one to two miles. Also known as a *crit*.

cross gearing—A configuration of front and rear gears that uses same-sized gear configurations, such as large chainring–large rear sprocket.

cyclocross—A type of off-road race using bicycles that resemble road bikes. Cyclocross courses are very rough and muddy and are designed to force the competitors to dismount and run with their bicycles several times per lap.

derailleur—A mechanism for moving the chain from one sprocket to another to change gears on a multi-speed bicycle.

disc brakes—Brakes that apply force to metal discs, called rotors, attached to the wheels to stop.

down tube—The frame tube that runs diagonally up from the front of the bottom bracket up to the lower end of the head tube.

drafting—Riding behind another cyclist to take advantage of reduced wind resistance.

drive train—The parts of a bicycle that have to do with generating forward motion. This would include the pedals, cranks, chain wheels, bottom bracket, chain, derailleurs, rear sprockets, and rear hub.

drop bars—Handlebars curved in the shape of a ram's horn.

follow-flat—A second flat that succeeds an improperly repaired flat.

front-wheel principle—A principle of stability; the stability of the bike is determined by the stability of the front wheel.

headset—The bearing assembly that connects the front fork to the frame and permits the fork to turn for steering and balancing.

hydration pack—A water pack, worn on the back, with a straw that mounts on the shoulder for easy access.

hypothermia—Subnormal temperature of the body.

indexed shifting—Shift controller with positive detents or click stops that provide discrete positions corresponding to different gears.

lock rings—Thin locknuts used to keep the threaded assembly from coming unscrewed.

mode share—The percentage share that a particular type of transportation mode (e.g., car, bus, rail, plane) has in relation to other modes.

mode-shift—Changing the form of transportation (e.g., from car to bicycle).

pacelining—Riding close behind other cyclists in a line so that each cyclist can draft the cyclist in front.

panniers—Bags mounted on a rack on the bike to carry gear.

pinch flat—Tube damage characterized by two small slits. This is usually caused by hitting a sharp edge such as a construction plate or pothole on underinflated tubes and pinching the tube against the rim. (Also called a *snakebite flat*.)

Presta—One of two types of valves that are commonly found on bicycle tubes. These valves are narrow, and you must unscrew a locknut before you can check tire pressure. Often used on high-pressure bicycle tires. (See also *Schrader*.)

psi—Pounds per square inch.

quick release—A cam mechanism that allows the wheels to be removed quickly and without any tools.

recumbent bike—A bike on which riders sit in a reclined, or recumbent, position and pedal with their legs in front of their body.

rim brakes—Brakes that apply force to the wheel rims to stop them from turning.

rock dodge—A maneuver for avoiding a small object in the road. To execute, once close to the obstruction, turn the handlebars quickly to one side (to avoid the object), and immediately straighten.

rpm—Revolutions per minute.

SAG (support and gear) wagon—Support and gear vehicle providing rider assistance on organized rides.

Schrader—One of two types of valves that are commonly found on bicycle tubes. These valves are wide, and you can check tire pressure without unscrewing anything. (See also *Presta*.)

seat post—The tubular support that holds the saddle.

shifters—The hand controls for a gear shifting system.

short-track racing—A multilap race that is relatively short and intense in comparison to the classic cross-country format.

snakebite flat—Tube damage characterized by two small slits. This is usually caused by hitting a sharp edge such as a construction plate or pothole on underinflated tubes and pinching the tube against the rim. (Also called a *pinch flat*.)

spoke wrench—Tool used to adjust the tightness of the spokes and keep the wheel true.

stem—The part that connects the handlebars to the steerer of the fork.

tire levers—Tools used to remove the tire bead from the rim.

toe clips—A type of pedal with a strap on it to strap your shoe to the pedal, providing better pedaling efficiency.

toe-in—Brake adjustment in which the front of the brake pad touches the rim first to reduce squealing.

true—The quality of a wheel in which the rim is perfectly concentric and runs along a plane perpendicular to the axle.

velodromes—Arenas for track cycling.

wattage meter—A device mounted on the bicycle that measures the power of the cyclist's output.

REFERENCES

Allen, J.S. 2001. Drafting and paceline riding. www.bikexprt.com/streetsmarts/usa/chapter7a.htm.

Allwood, M. 2007. *The complete do-it-yourself bike book: Everything you need to know to fix, maintain and get the most out of your bike.* London: Carlton Books.

American Association of State Highway and Transportation Officials. 1999. *Guide for the development of bicycle facilities.* Washington, DC: AASHTO.

Armstrong, L., & Carmichael, C. 2000. *The Lance Armstrong performance program: Seven weeks to the perfect ride.* Emmaus, PA: Rodale Press. Distributed by St. Martin's Press.

Bailey, D., & Gates, K. 2009. *Bike repair & maintenance for dummies.* Hoboken, NJ: Wiley.

Centers for Disease Control and Prevention. n.d. Trends in childhood obesity. www.cdc.gov/obesity/childhood/trends.html.

Cross, K.D., & Fisher, G. 1977. *A study of bicycle/motor-vehicle accidents: Identification of problem types and countermeasure approaches.* Volume 3—Coding index—Appendices E-G. Final report, DOT HS 803 317, September (PB 282572). Washington, DC: National Highway Traffic Safety Administration.

Did You Know? n.d. Bicycle facts. http://didyouknow.org/bicycles.

Federal Highway Administration. 1995, April. *Bicycle safety-related research synthesis.* Pub. No. FHWA-RD-94-062. Available: http://drusilla.hsrc.unc.edu/cms/downloads/BikeSafety-ResearchSynthesis1995.pdf.

Friel, J. 2009. *The cyclist's training bible.* Boulder, CO: Velo Press.

Goodman, J.D. 2010, January 31. An electric boost for bicyclists. *New York Times.* Available: www.bicyclelaw.com/news/n.cfm/an-electric-boost-for-bicyclists.

Henry J. Kaiser Family Foundation. 2010. Report: Generation M2: Media in the lives of 8- to 18-year-olds. www.kff.org/entmedia/8010.cfm.

International Mountain Bicycling Association. n.d. Rules of the trail. [Online]. www.imba.com/about/trail_rules.html [April 13, 2010].

Kaplan, J. 1975. *Characteristics of the regular adult bicycle user.* Unpublished master's thesis, University of Maryland.

Langley, J. 1999. *Bicycling Magazine's complete guide to bicycle maintenance and repair for road and mountain bikes.* Emmaus, PA: Rodale Press. Distributed by St. Martin's Press.

League of American Bicyclists. n.d. Five steps to riding better. www.bikeleague.org/resources/better/.

League of American Bicyclists. 2004. *The league guide to safe and enjoyable bicycling.* Washington, DC: League of American Bicyclists.

Moritz, W.E. 1998. Adult bicyclists in the United States: Characteristics and riding experience in 1996. *Transportation Research Record: Journal of the Transportation Research Board* 1636: 1-7.

National Bicycle Dealers Association. 2009. *U.S. bicycle market report.* Available: http://nbda.com.

National Highway Traffic Safety Administration. 2008. *Traffic safety facts: 2008 data.* DOT HS 811 156. Washington, DC: NHTSA. Available: www-nrd.nhtsa.dot.gov/pubs/811156.pdf.

NutriStrategy. 2005. Calories burned bike riding or cycling. www.nutristrategy.com/fitness/cycling.htm.

Pedestrian and Bicycle Information Center. n.d. Pedestrian and bicycle crash analysis tool. www.walkinginfo.org/facts/pbcat/index.cfm.

Sorenson, E., and the staff of Sightline Institute. 2008. Why bikes are a sustainable wonder, adapted from Sightline. 2006. *Seven Wonders.* www.sightline.org/research/sust_toolkit/solutions/bicycle.

U.S. Census Bureau. 2008. American Community Survey. Available at: www.census.gov/acs/www/index.html.

Zinn, L., & Telander, T. 2009. *Zinn and the art of road bike maintenance.* Boulder, CO: Velo Press.

INDEX

Note: Page numbers followed by italicized *f* or *ff* indicates a figure or multiple figures on those pages, respectively. Page numbers followed by an italicized *t* indicates a table on those pages.

ABOUT THE EDITOR

Andy Clarke is president of the League of American Bicyclists, where he has expanded the league's Smart Cycling program and developed the Bicycle Friendly America program. He has more than 25 years of experience in cycling advocacy, having worked with the Rails to Trails Conservancy and the Bicycle Federation of America (now the National Center for Bicycling and Walking). He was executive director of the Association of Pedestrian and Bicycle Professionals. He also served as a consultant to the Federal Highway Administration and coauthored the Administration's *Bicycle Safety-Related Research Synthesis*. From 1993 to 2002, he was on the Bicycle Transportation Committee of the Transportation Research Board of the National Academy of Sciences, serving as chair for the last three years.

Clarke is a founding member of America Bikes and the Association of Pedestrian and Bicycle Professionals. In 2003 he earned the Paul Dudley White Award from the American Heart Association for outstanding contributions to bicycling, and the Distinguished Service Award from the Association of Pedestrian and Bicycle Professionals.

Clarke's passion for cycling started when he was growing up in England and has stayed with him through hundreds of thousands of miles of cycling on four continents. He lives in Fairfax, Virginia, with his wife, Kristen, and his two children, Ashton and Jacqueline.

ABOUT THE ORGANIZATION

The League of American Bicyclists was founded as the League of American Wheelmen in 1880. In an effort to improve riding conditions so they might better enjoy their newly discovered sport, more than 100,000 cyclists from across the United States joined the league to advocate for paved roads. Today, the league's mission is to promote bicycling for fun, fitness, and transportation and to work through advocacy and education for a bicycle-friendly America. It works to achieve these goals through two programs: the Bicycle Friendly America program and the Smart Cycling program. The Bicycle Friendly America program recognizes communities, states, and businesses nationwide that support the five Es of bicycling: education, enforcement, engineering, evaluation, and encouragement. The Smart Cycling program is the United States' only nationwide instructor certification program. It teaches basic riding technique, safety skills, and bike maintenance, which allow riders to feel more comfortable on the road.

USING THE DVD

Smart Cycling, the DVD in this book, is an additional resource for learning and teaching cycling skills and safety. The DVD is meant to be played after you read the book (or while you read it) to further illustrate many of the concepts in the chapters. The main menu includes the following tracks:

- Essential Bicycling Skills (22:01): This video covers preparing to ride, riding safely, riding in traffic, negotiating road hazards, riding at night, and other tips. It shows cyclists in real-life situations and details the correct ways to interact with other vehicles. This video is best used in conjunction with a class taught by a league cycling instructor. Find classes in your area at www.bikeleague.org.
- Bicycle Safety Tips for Adults (7:23): This is a quick summary of the Essential Bicycling Skills video. It can serve as a refresher for people who have been off their bikes for a while or a good introduction to the topics covered in the longer video.

From the main menu, you can also select Additional Resources to go to a submenu that offers the following three tracks:

- Cyclist's-Eye View (20:26): This track uses a bike-mounted camera to follow a cyclist as he rides in traffic and interacts with other vehicles. The video explores some of the same techniques as the previous tracks, but with a different perspective.
- Kid's-Eye View (English) (10:22): Children and cycling are a wonderful match, but kids need to be taught how to ride safely in traffic. This video explores some of the common mistakes that they make while riding and teaches the correct techniques.
- Kid's-Eye View (Spanish) (11:04): This video is a Spanish-language version of the Kids'-Eye View.